you fix it:
Insulation

you fix it:
Insulation

Joseph Lo Schiavo & Frank Lo Cicero

in association with
Carmine C. Castellano & Clifford P. Seitz

ARCO
New York

HENNEPIN COUNTY LIBRARY

DEC 30 1977

Dedicated to Constance and Eleanor

Published by Arco Publishing Company, Inc.
219 Park Avenue South, New York, N.Y. 10003

Copyright © 1975 by Training Analysis and Products, Inc.

All rights reserved. No part of this book may be
reproduced, by any means, without permission in
writing from the publisher, except by a reviewer
who wishes to quote brief excerpts in connection
with a review in a magazine or newspaper.

Library of Congress Catalog Card Number 74-14206
ISBN 0-668-03614-1

Printed in the United States of America

CONTENTS

INTRODUCTION

This book has been expressly designed to provide the home owner and the prospective new or used home buyer with quick and simple methods for locating heating and cooling losses in the home. It explains what the home owner can do to minimize these losses and thus save money on his fuel bills and enjoy a more comfortable home in both winter and summer.

The rising cost of fuel can be substantially reduced by following the steps suggested and methods described in this book.

This book provides a means for making a dollar value trade-off, which tells the home owner whether it is economically feasible to correct a given condition or if the cost of the remedy will be more than the savings realized.

By following the check procedures given, the reader will realize an added benefit to combating rising costs of fuel: he will give his home a thorough inspection for quality of construction, especially areas involved with heat loss.

This book is divided into sections, each giving a step-by-step check procedure to follow. These checks lead the do-it-yourself home owner to his insulation problem, if there is one, and indicates the available solution.

Section 1000 locates the most probable area of heating losses and gives means to substantially minimize the losses;

Section 2000 helps the home owner to actually calculate the dollar cost of his fuel heating loss;

Section 3000 presents dollar value of the method employed to minimize the heating loss versus potential dollar gain from the reduced amount of fuel consumed; and

Section 4000 suggests summer and winter maintenance procedures.

ISOLATING HEAT LOSS LOCATIONS IN THE HOUSE

SECTION 1000

DOORS AND DOOR ENTRY HEAT LOSSES

FAULT SYMPTOM 1010

Possible Causes:

Initial Conditions Check List:

a. Perform these checks on a cool or cold windy day with a strong breeze blowing. This will help to make it easy to find air leaks.

b. When running these checks on doors, be sure any outer storm door is propped fully open. If storm door is closed leaks may be very hard to locate.

1011

Nonexistent or faulty weatherseals

The primary cause of heat loss at exterior doors and entryways is lack of weatherstripping or improper application of weathersealants (see Fig. 1). Heat loss that is attributed to these conditions can range from five to ten percent of the total fuel costs. To establish whether these conditions exist proceed to Step 1.

Fig. 1. Checking for faulty or missing weather-stripping.

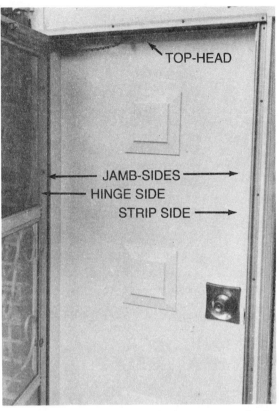

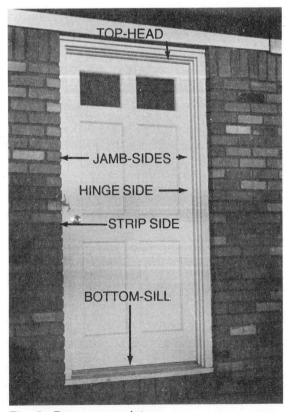

Fig. 2. Door nomenclature.

Step 1—Give the door and its surrounding frame a cursory visual examination. If there is no weatherstripping, proceed to Step 3. See Fig. 2. This step is particularly important to the novice you-fix-it handyman. Take a few moments to study the figure and notes and become familiar with the entire door assembly and its component parts. Take special notice that the top of the door assembly is called the "head," the sides the "jambs," and the bottom the "sill." These parts will be referred to in the steps which follow.

Step 2—From the interior of the house,

with the interior door in the closed position, carefully examine the seams at the head, jams, and sill. Look for light penetration from the exterior. If in doubt darken the room by drawing blinds, shades, etc.

Can light be seen to penetrate at the head or jambs?

YES—Penetrating light at the head or jambs is most often caused by faulty weatherstripping. Light penetration also means air penetrates. Cold winter air entering the home results in dollar loss. Proceed to Step 3.

NO—Weatherstripping may be in satisfactory condition. Proceed to Step 3.

Does light penetrate at the sill?

YES—Light penetration means faulty weatherstripping. Proceed to Step 3.

NO—Sills appear to be in satisfactory condition. For further verification proceed to Step 3.

Step 3—Use a piece of soft flexible paper or very light tissue, or use the palm of your hand and trace over the door seams at the head, jambs, and sill, as in Fig. 3. Your hand will feel, or a gentle blowing of the tissue will establish the fact, that air is actually penetrating through these seams (see Fig. 4). A substantial amount of air can enter along these points, even though light

penetration was not evident. Bear in mind that a building cannot be airtight; it must breathe. Therefore, some very small amount of air can be acceptable. This small amount should be barely noticeable with the palm of your hand. The tissue should not wave as in a breeze.

Does there appear to be a moderate or even heavy air penetration along any of the seams?

Fig. 3. Check the interior of the door head with tissue paper for air penetrations.

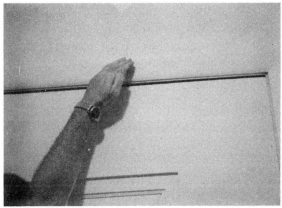

Fig. 4. Using the palm of the hand, check the door for air penetrations.

YES—This indicates that the weatherseal is either defective or pieces are missing. Proceed to Step 4.

NO—Weatherseals appear to be in satisfactory condition. Continue to Step 4 for additional checks.

Step 4—Close the door and look at it from the outside. Carefully examine the head, jambs, and sill to determine whether the weatherstripping and doorstops are tight to the face of the door. See Fig. 2. Are both the weatherstripping and doorstops firmly against the face of the door?

YES—The weatherseals appear to be in satisfactory condition. Any heat loss at these particular points should be minimal. Proceed to **1012.**

NO—When doorstops and weatherstripping are not firmly placed against the face of the door, these problems are added causes of heat loss at the door. These conditions could also account for the light penetration. For correction of these weatherstripping maladies and improperly fitting doorstops, refer to a book on carpentry or consult your local lumber dealer. Continue to **1012** for further heat-loss checks.

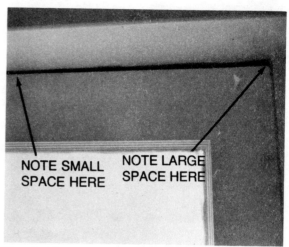

Fig. 5. Visual examination of head shows that door is improperly hung and needs adjustment.

YES—Either an upper or lower hinge on the door has come loose. This space formed by the door hanging askew has greatly reduced the usefulness of any weatherstripping. Proceed to Step 2 for further verification of an improperly hung door.

NO—If the door seams appear to be evenly spaced and tight to the head, sill, and jambs, then the door has been properly hung. For a final check proceed to Step 2.

Step 2—Open the door about halfway. Place yourself facing the edge of the door (see Fig. 6). Hold the door by the knob and press the door toward the hinged side. This procedure checks whether the hinges or fasteners are loose.

Does the door rock back and forth to any appreciable degree?

1012

Door is improperly hinged

Step 1—Examine the seams of the door from the inside of the house with the door closed to see if it hangs straight (see Fig. 5).

Does the door appear to rub the jamb on the latch side at either the top or the bottom?

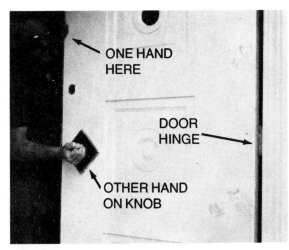

Fig. 6. Test door by applying pressure toward the hinge side.

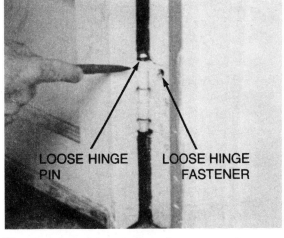

Fig. 7. Loose hinge pins or fasteners will cause the door to hang badly and rock back and forth.

YES—This is a certain indication that one or more of the hinge fasteners has come loose. Check the screw fastenings on the hinges and the hinge pins. Sometimes the pins work themselves loose or they may have been improperly mounted. See Fig. 7. Correction for this fault is simple. Tighten the loose screw fasteners or fully insert the hinge pin properly. Now proceed to **1013** for additional checks of heat loss.

NO—Proceed to **1013** for a continuation of heat-loss checks.

1013

Door and/or frame are poorly constructed

Step 1—The exterior and interior sides of the door and doorframe should be examined very carefully. Examine the door first. Look for cracks in the door panels and for poor jointing at the corners. Cracks in the face of the door panels or loose or poor jointing will allow entry of cold air, thus causing heat loss.

Is there evidence of cracking, looseness, or poor construction of joints?

YES—Heat is escaping at these points. These faults can be corrected by caulking and repainting. See Fig. 8. Proceed to Step 2 for additional checks.

NO—Proceed to Step 2 for continuation of heat-loss checks.

Step 2—The body of the door may be of such poor construction as to render it inefficient when used as an exterior weather door. Checking this is simple. Tap the face of the door in its center, listening to hear if it is solid or hollow (see Fig. 9). A hollow metal

Fig. 8. Caulk and repaint open joints to conserve fuel.

Fig. 9. Tap the door to determine if it is solidly constructed for use as an exterior door.

door used as an entry door is a very inefficient weather door.

Does the door sound as though it is hollow?

YES—The remedy for this condition is to replace the door with one of solid construction. Consult your local lumber dealer for a suitable replacement door. Proceed to Step 3 for further heat-loss checks.

NO—Proceed to Step 3 for additional checks.

Step 3—A final check of the door is to thoroughly examine the doorframe. Carefully examine the head, sill, and jambs of the doorframe. Look for major sepa-

rations in the framework and severe deterioration of the frame material. This examination should be performed on both the interior and exterior sides of the entry door. Drafts enter the home via separations in the framework or through deteriorated material.

Is there any evidence of these faults in the frame?

YES—This condition is the major cause of heat loss at the door. It should be corrected immediately. Consult a carpenter or your local lumber dealer. Proceed to **1014**.

NO—Proceed to **1014** for other heat-loss checks.

NOTE GAP AND
IMPROPER SEAL

Fig. 10. A gap at the storm door head can cause very costly fuel consumption.

1014

Nonexistent or incorrect installation of storm door units.

Step 1—Heat loss at the door location is greatly increased when a storm door unit is not installed. Not only does the storm door save heat, but it also protects the basic house door and entryway from rain, snow, and sleet. For those entryways where storm door units already exist, proceed to Step 2. See Fig. 10.

Step 2—From the interior side of the storm door unit, with the storm door in the closed position, carefully examine the seams at the head, jambs, and sill. Check particularly for light penetrating from the exterior.

Is light penetrating at the head or jambs?

YES—Weatherstripping on the storm door is faulty or missing. Wherever light is penetrating cold air is also penetrating. Proceed to Step 3.

NO—Weatherstripping appears to be in satisfactory condition. For further verification, proceed to Step 3.

Does light appear to be penetrating at the sill?

YES—Faulty or nonexistent weatherstripping. Proceed to Step 3.

NO—Proceed to Step 3.

Step 3—Using the palm of the hand, trace over the seams of the storm door at the head, jambs, and sill. Bear in mind that the storm door unit will not be absolutely airtight. However, the air penetrating should be almost minimal.

Is the air flowing in moderate or heavy?

YES—Weatherseals are either faulty or missing. Proceed to Step 4 for a continued check. Correction of this condition requires servicing of the storm door.

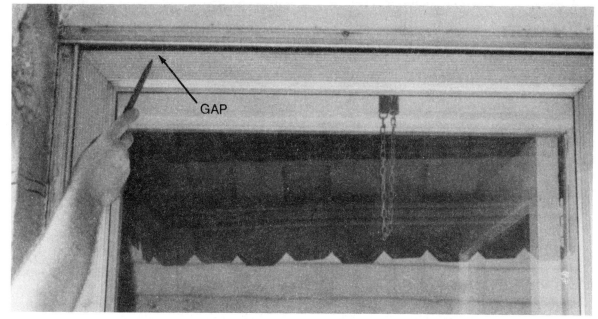

Fig. 11. The weatherseal is not sitting as tightly against storm door at head as it is at the jambs, causing a gap.

NO—Proceed to Step 4 for continuation of heat-loss checks.

Step 4—With the storm door in the closed position, and from the outside of the storm door, carefully examine the head, jambs, and sill of the storm unit to ascertain that the weatherseals and doorstops are sitting smugly against the face of the storm door (see Fig. 11).

Are the storm door stops and weatherseals firmly against the face of the storm door?

YES—Proceed to **1015**.

NO—These faults greatly reduce the efficiency of the storm door unit and cause an excessive and unnecessary loss of heat. This condition also verifies the light penetration test as performed in Step 2. Proceed to **1015**.

1015

Caulking is faulty or was improperly applied

Step 1—From the exterior side of the house, examine the juncture of the entryway and door framework with the main building. Especially look for loose or missing sections of caulking (see Fig. 12).

Are there loose or missing sections of caulking?

YES—These could be causing drafts to enter the house through the framework and should be replaced. Refer to Fig. 13. Proceed to Step 2 for additional checks.

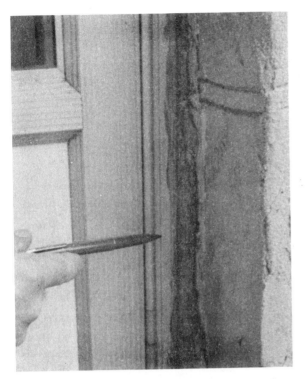

Fig. 12. Loose or cracked caulking at the door could cause heavy draft to be felt inside the house.

Fig. 13. Apply caulking to the door frame after removal of loose and cracked caulking.

NO—Proceed to Step 2.

Step 2—Some entranceways to homes have glazed (glass-framed) side panels at the doors or vestibules. These glazed side panels should be carefully checked in a manner similar to that previously described for the door and framework. Refer to **1020**.

Step 3—Up to this point the door and surrounding framework have been given a thorough check against heat loss. Keep in mind that air circulation cannot be entirely eliminated. However, the quantity of air that enters should be so small that the home owner will be hard put to discover its point of entry. Should a substantial amount of air still be entering the house, repeat **1011** through **1015**.

WINDOW HEAT LOSSES

FAULT SYMPTOM 1020

Possible Causes:

- Nonexistent or faulty weatherseals ——————— **See 1021**
- Window and/or frame are poorly constructed ————————————— **See 1022**

- Nonexistent or incorrect installation of storm window units ——————— **See 1023**
- Caulking ———————————————— **See 1024**
- Thermal glazing (thermo-panes) ————— **See 1025**

Fig. 14. Familiarize yourself with the nomenclature for window components. The names are the same for both the window interior and exterior.

Fig. 15. Broken glass should be replaced immediately, both as a safety measure and for fuel economy.

Initial Conditions Check List:

a. Perform these checks on a cool or cold day when there is a strong breeze blowing. This will make it easier to find possible air leaks quickly.

b. When running these checks on windows, be sure any outer storm window is propped fully open. If storm window is closed, leaks may be hard to locate.

1021

Nonexistent or faulty weatherseals

Step 1—Examine the window to become familiar with its component parts and proper nomenclature (see Fig 14). These window parts names will be referred to and used in the stops which follow.

Step 2—Stand in front of the window and scan it to see if any glazing (glass) is missing or broken (see Fig. 15).

Is any glass cracked, punctured, or broken?

YES—Replace the glass. Proceed to Step 3.

Fig. 16. Use a light piece of tissue paper to test for air penetrations. Be sure any storm unit is open prior to testing.

NO—Proceed to Step 3 and continue examination of the window unit.

Step 3—Put the window in the closed position. Be sure that if there is a storm window it is open, or that it is in the up position. Check the window for air penetration. Using a piece of light tissue paper or the palm of your hand, trace along the seams at the head, sill, and jambs. Take special care to trace along all the mullions and muttons of multi-paned window units (see Fig. 16). Air penetrating at any of these points will result in isolation of a key area in your check.

MISSING, BENT, OR BROKEN WEATHERSEALS

Fig. 17. Air penetrations at the window are often caused by faulty weatherseals.

Does air penetrate anywhere along the head, jambs, sill, or other seams?

YES—A probable cause is that one or more of the weatherseals is faulty or nonexistent. Refer to Fig. 17 and then continue to Step 4 for additional checks.

NO—Proceed to Step 4.

Keep in mind that a window cannot be 100 percent airtight. Operating sections of the window have joints. These joints are weatherproof but not airtight. However, it is important that the amount of air penetrating through the window unit should be minimal and almost unnoticed as you perform this test.

Fig. 18. Check these points for loose or shaky frame and glass jointing.

Fig. 19. Missing portions of glazing compound create a hazardous condition that should be remedied immediately.

Step 4—After checking the window unit for points of air penetration, examine the glass panels and frame. Check to see if the window unit frame joints or the glass pane jointing is loose, shaky, or deteriorated. Particularly check along the edges of the glass panels for any signs of deterioration. See Figs. 18 and 19 for guidelines.

Are any of the window frame joints or glazing joints loose or deteriorated?

YES—This fault should be corrected immediately. This condition constitutes a safety hazard particularly for small children. Refer to Fig. 20 for guidelines.

NO—Proceed to Step 5 for a continuation of examination.

Step 5—Now check the window from the exterior side. In cases where it is not possible for the do-it-yourself home owner to reach the windows or there is no ladder to reach high windows, etc., then the use of binoculars is suggested. If the window is large enough, the frame, etc. can be checked from the interior (see Fig. 21). Repeat the visual examination of Step 4 from the exterior side of the window.

Are the framework or glass in poor condition?

YES—The frame or glass requires correction.

NO—Then proceed to **1022** for continuation of heat-loss checks at the windows.

Fig. 20. Loose joints of the window frame and cracked glass panes should be repaired immediately.

1022

Window and/or frame are poorly constructed

Step 1—Examine the window unit and its surrounding framework at both the interior and exterior sides (see Figs. 22 and 23). Look for deterioration such as splitting, rotting, crumbly wood, etc. If there are multiple layers of paint or varnish over the window unit then use a sharp pointed tool such as an awl or small screwdriver. Gently, but firmly, push down on the frame and also the surrounding framework at random points (see Figs. 24 and 25).

Fig. 21. When exterior examination of a large window is not possible, open window wide and sit on the ledge. Holding onto window frame, examine window.

Fig. 22. Examine the window frame interior at these check points.

Fig. 23. Examine the window exterior at these check points.

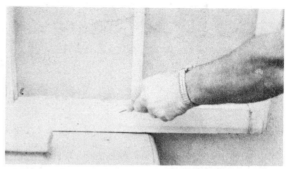

Fig. 24. Check the exterior of the window frame for deterioration.

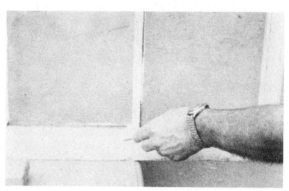

Fig. 25. Use a sharp, pointed tool to check the interior of the window frame for damage.

Is there evidence of loose jointing or deterioration of the framework construction?

YES—Replace or repair the jointing or framework. See Figs. 24 and 26. Then continue to Step 2 for additional checks.

NO—Proceed to Step 2 for continued checks.

Step 2—In cases where the frame appears to be solid and well constructed, but air is penetrating, the most likely cause is that the glass panels have poor, aged glazing or were improperly glazed. From the exterior side, look closely at the condition of the glazing compound along the edges of the glass panes (see Fig. 27). Especially look for dried out or missing portions of the glazing compound as shown in the figure.

Is the glazing compound in poor condition, or are large sections missing?

YES—This is a major cause of air penetration at the window unit. Loose glass panes are also subject to being torn away from the window unit during high winds. For correction of this condition, refer to Figs. 28 and 29. Proceed to **1023** for additional checks.

Fig. 26. A deteriorated bottom sash can be finished to match an existing upper sash.

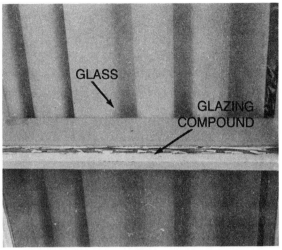

Fig. 27. Check the condition of glazing compound and glass for cracks and missing sections.

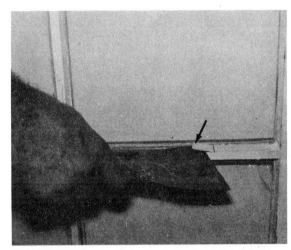

Fig. 28. Remove damaged glazing compound.

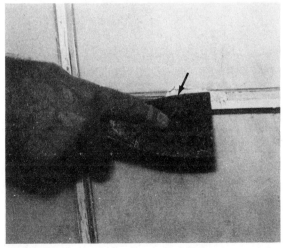

Fig. 29. Add new glazing compound to glass pane.

NO—Proceed to **1023** for continued checks of heat loss at the window unit.

1023

Nonexistent or incorrect installation of storm window units

Step 1—Open the window. If there is no storm window, refer to **2000** for information on heating fuel loss. Carefully examine the storm window to determine whether the storm unit glazing and screening are in good condition. See Fig. 21.

Is there a storm window unit?

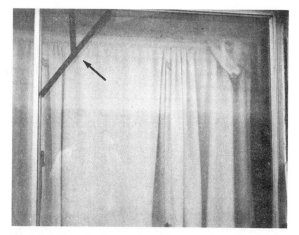

Fig. 30. Taping should be placed at both sides of broken glass panes prior to removing the unit and taking it to a professional glazier.

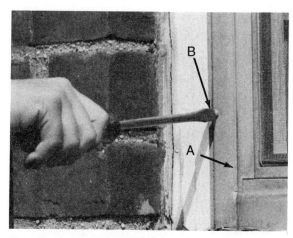

Fig. 31. Loose storm window frames (A) should be secured tightly (B) to prevent air penetration.

Are the glass panes damaged?

YES—For glass replacement, refer to Fig. 30 for guidelines. Proceed to Step 2.

NO—Proceed to Step 2 for additional checks.

Step 2—With the storm window in the closed position, examine the head, sill, and jambs for strong, penetrating air currents. Air entry should be almost impossible to discern.

Is air penetrating through the storm window unit so that it can be easily felt?

YES—Check to be sure the storm window is completely closed. Then check for a loose storm unit frame. If the frame is loose, secure it tightly (see Fig. 31 for guidelines). Continue to **1024**.

NO—Storm window appears to be airtight. Proceed to **1024**.

1024

Caulking

Step 1—From the exterior side of the window unit examine the head, sill, and jambs of the frame where they meet the building. Look for loose, cracked, or missing sections of caulking (see Figs. 32 and 33).

Does caulking appear to be in good condition?

YES—Proceed to Step 2.

NO—Faulty caulking means air entry through the framework. See Fig. 34 for recaulking the window. Proceed to Step 2.

Step 2—Up to this point the window, window frame, and storm unit have been examined for points of air penetration and heat loss. In the event that cold air is felt near the

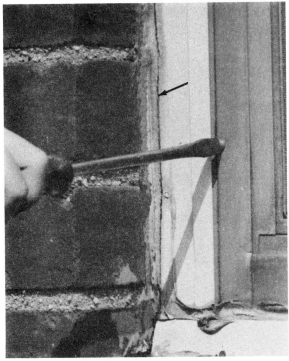

Fig. 32. Securing a frame which has cracked caulking and open seams will not completely solve the problem.

Fig. 33. Missing portions of cracked and loose caulking should be remedied immediately.

inside of windows, the you-fix-it home owner is advised to re-trace the steps of **1021–1024** for possible oversights.

1025

Thermal glazing (thermo-panes)

The you-fix-it home owner who has ther-mal glazed window units in his home should proceed to check these units for heat losses as follows:

Step 1—Weatherseals, window units, and frames should be checked as in **1021** and **1022.**

Step 2—Storm units and caulking should be checked as in **1023** and **1024.**

Fig. 34. When applying caulking with gun, fill in all voids.

ATTIC LOSSES OF HEAT

FAULT SYMPTOM 1030

Possible Causes:

- No insulation; unfinished attic ——————— See 1031
- Eaves, defects ——————————————— See 1032
- Roofing defects, flat roof —————————— See 1033
- Attic windows ———————————————— See 1034
- Attic entry and exit doors ————————— See 1035

Initial Conditions Check Lits:

a. Perform these checks on a cool or cold day when there is a strong breeze blowing. This makes it easier to locate air-leak sources.

b. Stand near the house-side of the attic and note whether or not there are drafts or breezes which can be felt.

c. When running these checks on attic windows, be sure that any outer storm window is propped fully open.

1031

No insulation; unfinished attic

The primary cause of heat loss from this attic is no insulation. The following checks apply only to an unfinished attic. For heat-loss checks on finished attics, refer to **1032–1035**. Take a few moments to study Fig. 35 and its notes to become familiar with the entire attic and the nomenclature of its parts.

Step 1—A quick visual examination of the attic will reveal whether or not there is insulation.

Has insulation been installed? Is it in good condition? Refer to Fig. 36 for guidelines.

YES—Proceed to Step 2.

NO—See Fig. 37 for installation guidelines. Also, refer to manufacturers' installation instructions.

Step 2—If insulation is installed in the attic floor, follow this step. If it is installed in the rafters, proceed to Step 3. Examine the floor beams, all the way out to outside building walls. Be certain that the insulation is properly fitted, sealing the entire length of the floor beams (see Fig. 37).

Is insulation properly applied along the beams to the outer walls?

YES—Proceed to Step 3.

NO—Insulation should be installed throughout the attic floor beam area all the way out to the outer walls. Refer to Fig. 37. Then proceed to Step 3.

Step 3—If insulation is installed in the rafters, proceed with this step. Examine the rafters. Especially look for missing sections or large gaps in the insulation.

Is insulation installed throughout the rafter area, and is in good condition?

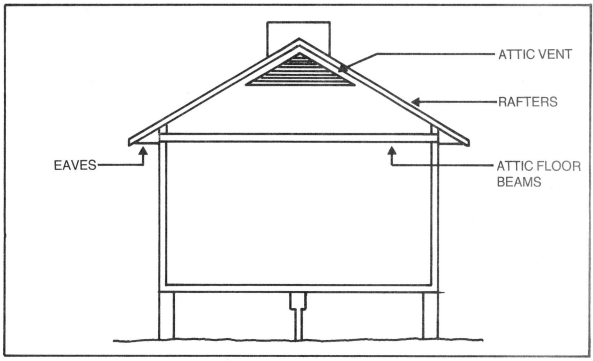

Fig. 35. Become familiar with the nomenclature of attic components before proceeding further with the inspection.

YES—Heat loss at this location is not a problem. For further heat-loss checks proceed to **1032**.

NO—Refer to Fig. 38 for installation guidelines. For additional heat-loss checks proceed to **1032**.

1032

Eaves, defects

Heat loss from the attic can become a serious problem if the eaves are not properly insulated and if they are not being used for proper attic air circulation. Fuel can be wasted and water and ice problems can result when the eaves are not properly insulated.

Step 1—Perform a visual examination of the attic eaves from inside the attic. If there are no louvers or vents at either end of the attic, high up near the ridgepole, then the eaves are being used for air circulation into the attic.

Are the eaves being used for air circulation?

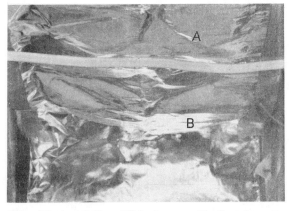

Fig. 36. Insulation (A) between attic floor beams (B).

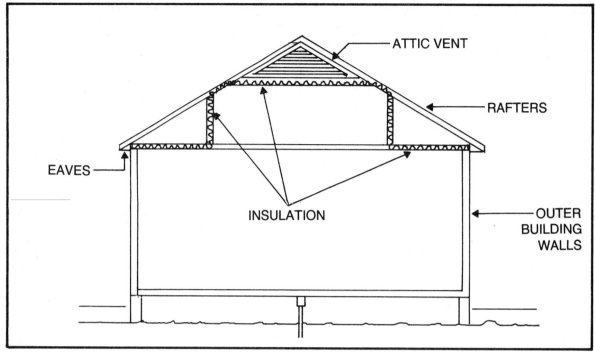

Fig. 37. Insulation should be applied all around portion of the attic that is habited. Extend insulation out to building walls at attic floor beams.

Fig. 38. Add required insulation to rafters.

YES—The eaves area can be insulated against heat loss, but it must be insulated in a manner which permits air to enter and circulate through the attic (see Fig. 39).

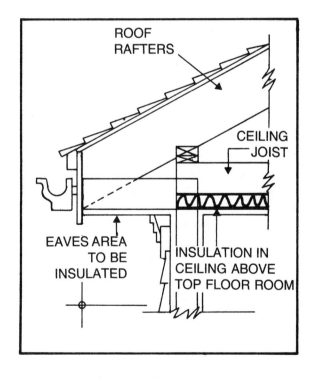

Fig. 39. Insulation should be installed in the eaves area and continued over top floor room.

NO—Air circulation is provided through the wall or through roof louvers. The eaves, therefore, can be made airtight. Refer to Fig. 40 for guidelines, and proceed to Step 2.

Step 2—Using a light piece of tissue paper or the palm of your hand, trace along all the edges of the eaves and soffit joints. (Note the location of the soffit in Fig 42). The tissue will help to establish if any excessive air is penetrating. Air penetration means heat loss.

Is there any excessive air penetrating?

YES—This condition can be corrected simply by caulking the open joint, provided that the open joint is not too large. Caulking will only yield an efficient seal on openings of a maximum of approximately ¼ inch in width. See Fig. 34 for use of a caulking gun.

NO—Refer to Step 1 to be sure that insulation is provided and properly installed.

1033

Roofing defects, flat roof

Roofs may be a cause of heat losses, particularly when they are not properly insulated or when openings and penetrations in the roof are poorly constructed or not maintained. This can allow an unnecessary amount of air into the house. Such defects consume fuel and can add to discomfort in the house. Proceed to Step 1.

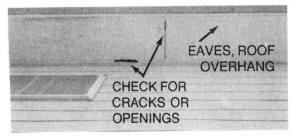

Fig. 40. Because these eaves are not providing air ventilation to the attic above, they should be repaired to produce an airtight condition.

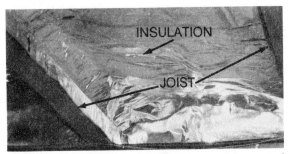

Fig. 41. Insulation installed between roof beams.

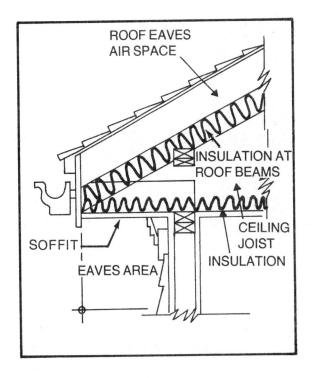

Fig. 42. Insulation should be provided throughout the attic when habited.

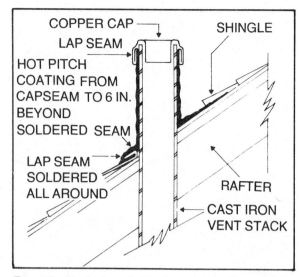

Fig. 43. Typical seal at a pipe penetrating a roof.

Step 1—Visual examination of the top floor ceiling is an easy check on whether sufficient insulation has been applied. Look for patchy areas of dust adhering to the ceiling, showing uneven heat areas.

Is there evidence that the roof is sufficiently insulated?

YES—Proceed to step 2.

NO—Installation is recommended. Refer to **2000** for estimated dollar costs and fuel dollar savings. For a recommended installation procedure, refer to Figs. 41 and 42, and also to manufacturers' installation instructions. Then proceed to Step 2.

Step 2—From the outside of the house, up on the roof, carefully examine all piping that is penetrating the roof, such as toilet vents, air vents, etc. Check particularly for water stains on the ceilings below, which are caused by water leakage into the ceiling from the roof. Where water enters air also enters, and heat is lost through these openings.

Is there evidence of water or air penetration?

YES—Refer to Fig. 43 for guidelines for applying sealant to piping and duct penetrations. Proceed to Step 3.

NO—Proceed to Step 3 for additional heat-loss checks.

Step 3—In cases where roofs are equipped with skylights, these skylights should be checked for airtightness. Carefully examine all the seams around the skylights. Refer to **1010** to perform these checks.

Are the skylights airtight?

YES—Proceed to Step 4 for continued checking of heat losses at the roof.

NO—Weatherstripping around the skylight requires replacement, or the skylight lacks caulking or insulation. See Fig. 44 for instructions. Proceed to Step 4.

Step 4—In many houses, exhaust fans are mounted in the roof. These fan installations should be sealed off to prevent excessive cold air from penetrating into the house. A careful visual examination will reveal if the fan

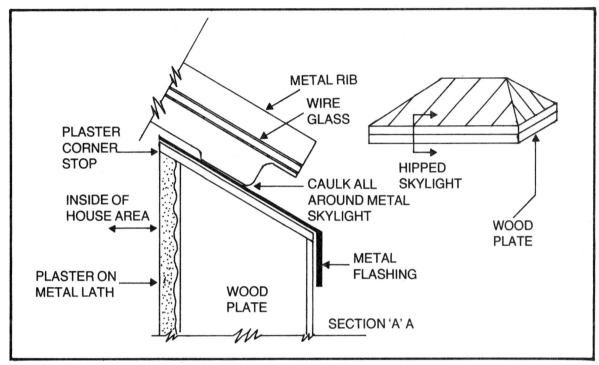

Fig. 44. Caulking should be applied all around skylight.

openings are sealed. Look for cracks or gaps between the fan housing and the roof.

Is there evidence of air penetrating at these exhaust fan locations?

YES—Openings at the fan housing base should be caulked. Refer to Fig. 45 for instructions and to **1010**. If the fan is not used during the winter, a removable cover can be installed over the fan housing. Proceed to **1034** for continued heat-loss checking.

NO—Proceed to **1034**.

1034

Attic windows

Attic windows can be a major cause of

Fig. 45. Missing caulking (arrows) causes costly fuel bills.

heat loss from the attic. These windows should be treated and serviced in the same manner as windows in the rest of the house. Thoroughly check the attic windows for heat loss by following the check steps of **1020**. Proceed to **1035** for continued heat-loss checks within the attic.

1035

Attic entry and exit doors

Doors are also a major cause of heat loss from the attic. Attic doors should be treated and serviced in the same manner as the home's main entrance doors. To thoroughly check these doors for heat loss, follow the detailed check steps of section **1010**. The steps and procedures followed up to this point have given the attic a thorough check for heat losses. If drafty cold from the attic can still be felt, it is recommended that the do-it-yourself home owner retrace the checks of **1031–1035**.

CONVENIENCE OPENINGS WHICH LOSE HEAT

FAULT SYMPTOM 1040

Possible Causes:

- Air conditioning units in the walls ———————— See **1041**
- Trap doors and scuttles ———————————— See **1042**
- Exterior accessory penetrations ——————— See **1043**

Initial Conditions Check List:

a. Perform these checks on a cool or cold day when a strong breeze is blowing. This will make it easier to locate air leaks.

b. When running these checks on any exterior cellar entrances, be sure that any outer storm units are propped fully open. If the storm unit is closed, air leaks will be difficult to locate.

c. An initial simple and quick check step is to stand on the house-side of the convenience opening and take note of any excessive drafts or breezes before beginning more detailed checks.

1041

Air conditioning units in the walls

Air leakage from through-the-wall air conditioning units can be a major cause of excessive fuel consumption. The following simple steps will assist the you-fix-it home owner in determining heat loss quickly.

Step 1—A visual examination from the exterior of the house will reveal whether air conditioning unit winter covers have been installed over any air conditioner.

Are there covers installed?

YES—Proceed to Step 2 for continued heat-loss checking.

NO—Install air conditioning winter covers. See Figs. 46 and 47 for guidelines, and refer to the cover manufacturers' installation instructions. Then proceed to Step 2.

Step 2—From the interior side of the house, use the palm of your hand or a piece of soft tissue paper to trace around all the edges and seams of the air conditioning unit. This will allow you to determine if there are excessive air penetrations at this location (see Fig. 48).

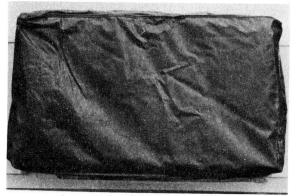

Fig. 46. Through-window air conditioner plastic cover.

Fig. 47. Through-window air conditioner units with (A) and without (B) covers.

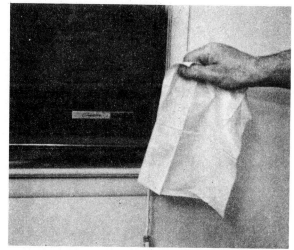

Fig. 48. Use the tissue test to check for air penetration.

Fig. 49. Sealant should be installed along seams.

Is there evidence of heavy air penetration?

YES—Air penetration is caused by a faulty seal between the air conditioning unit sleeve or unit housing and the main house wall. This condition is corrected simply by replacing the seal. Refer to Fig. 49 for guidelines. Then proceed to **1042** for additional heat-loss checking.

NO—If seals appear to be in satisfactory condition, proceed to **1042.**

1042

Trap doors and scuttles

See Figs. 50 and 51 for reference information on trap doors and scuttles locations.

Step 1—From the interior side of the trap doors or scuttle, place yourself directly in front of these units and determine if any excessive air drafts exist at these particular openings.

Fig. 50. Trap door in ceiling.

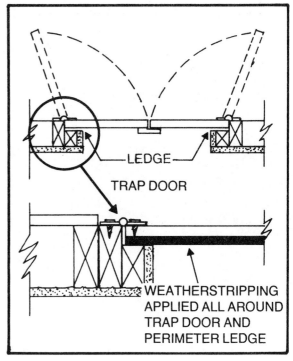

Fig. 52. Trap door or scuttle weatherstripping.

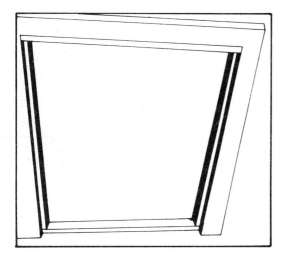

Fig. 51. Scuttle opening.

Are any excessive drafts evident?

YES—These drafts must be eliminated. Proceed to Step 2 for a more specific check.

NO—Proceed to Step 2 for additional heat-loss checking.

Step 2—Perform a visual examination of these units to establish whether there is evidence of faulty construction at large seams or gaps

or if parts have come loose from the unit (see Figs. 51 and 52).

Is there evidence of defects or damage?

YES—The unit should be replaced or repaired. For units that appear to be repairable, consult your local building supply dealer for repair guidance. Proceed to Step 3 for continued heat-loss checking.

NO—Proceed to Step 3 for additional heat-loss checking.

Step 3—From the interior side of the trap doors and scuttles, use the palm of your hand or a piece of soft tissue paper to trace around all the seams, particularly where the unit opens, and check for air drafts.

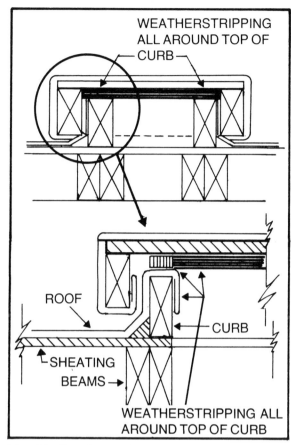

Fig. 53. Scuttle weatherstripping.

Is there evidence of air penetration?

YES—This indicates that weatherstripping has not been installed or that it needs to be replaced in order to eliminate the air penetration. Refer to Figs. 52 and 53 for instructions and guidelines. Proceed to **1043** for a continuation of heat-loss location checks.

NO—If the trap and scuttle units appear to be in satisfactory condition, proceed to **1043.**

1043

Exterior accessory penetrations

Air leaks at accessory penetrations into

Fig. 54. Typical fresh air intake vent. Arrow shows missing caulking.

Fig. 55. Dryer vent. Arrow shows caulking.

the house, such as pipes and electric lines, are problems that can be remedied simply. Fresh air intake pipes, pipes for hose bibbs, air vents, dryer vents, etc., are all examples of leak points (see Figs. 54–56).

Fig. 56. Electric cable (arrow).

Fig. 57. Install insulation and then caulk at convenience openings (A).

Step 1—From the interior of the house, check around all the accessory penetrations for air leakage. Use the palm of your hand or a piece of light tissue paper to trace around all seams, edges, or openings. This will enable you to establish if any air leaks are present.

Is air entering from around the accessory penetrations?

YES—Insulate these openings (see Fig. 57). Be sure to apply any required finish over the insulation so as to match the existing condition. Proceed to Step 2 and then to **1050.**

NO—Proceed to **1050** for additional heat-loss check steps.

All the house convenience openings have been given a thorough check for heat losses. Should a problem still exist, retrace the steps of **1041–1043.** Something may have been overlooked.

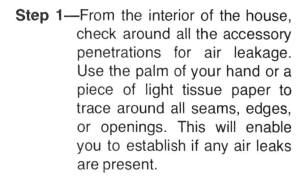

A
B

Fig. 58. Caulking accessory penetrations.
(A) Missing sealant at this penetration.
(B) Sealant should be as in this penetration.

HEAT LOSS FROM THE BASEMENT

FAULT SYMPTOM 1050

Possible Causes:

- Ceiling losses ——————————————— See 1051
- Basement wall losses ———————————— See 1052
- Basement window losses ——————————— See 1053
- Basement door losses ———————————— See 1054

Initial Conditions Check List:

a. Perform these checks on a cool or cold day when there is a strong breeze blowing. This will help make it easier to locate air leaks.

b. Perform a simple basement heat-loss check. Stand on the house-side of the basement. Take notice of any excessive drafts or breezes before beginning detailed checks.

c. When running these checks on windows or doors, be sure that any outer storm unit is propped fully open. If storm unit is closed, air leaks will be very difficult to locate.

1051

Ceiling losses

Air penetrating around the basement ceiling is often undetected. Air entering at the point where the beams of the floor above rest on the exterior foundation wall is a condition which is commonly overlooked. This is a cause of heat loss. The following checks are for an unfinished basement and will aid the you-fix-it home owner in locating any heat-loss problem areas. See Fig. 60 for guidelines.

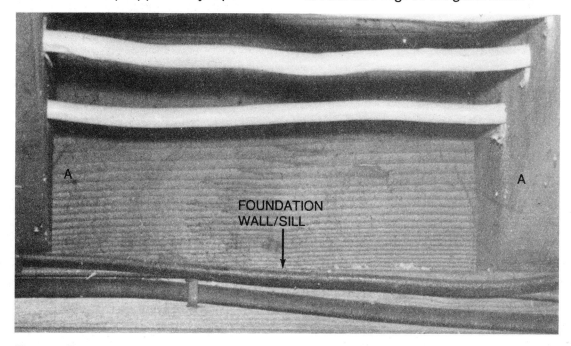

FOUNDATION
WALL/SILL

Fig. 59. Basement ceiling should be insulated at ends of floor beams (A).

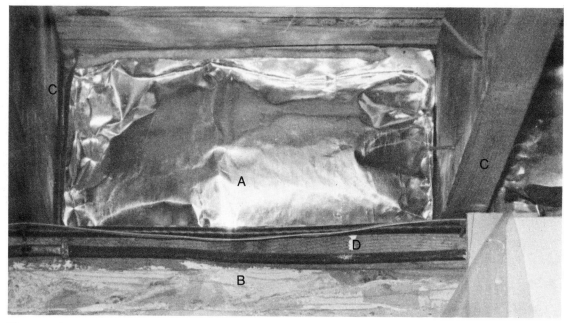

Fig. 60. Proper insulation (A) at basement ceiling and foundation wall juncture (B). Floor beams are (C); sill (D).

Step 1—From inside the basement, use the palm of your hand or a piece of soft tissue paper and follow all round the perimeter of the house at the line where the ceiling beams meet the walls. This line is called the sill.

Is air felt to be penetrating at the sill?

YES—Insulation must be installed between the floor beams and the underside of the floor, all around the top of the foundation wall. Refer to Fig. 61 and to manufacturers' installation instructions for guidelines. Proceed to Step 2.

NO—Sill appears to be airtight. Continue to Step 2.

Step 2—See Fig. 60. Proper sill insulation is extremely advantageous is maintaining an even temperature for the lowest fuel cost.

Carpeting on the floor above is also helpful as a temperature control. Proceed to **1052** for additional heat-loss check points.

1052
Basement wall losses

Basement walls can be sources of severe heat loss. In most houses the basement walls are uninsulated. The walls

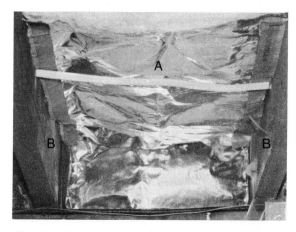

Fig. 61. Proper basement ceiling insulation (A). Floor beams in basement ceiling are marked (B).

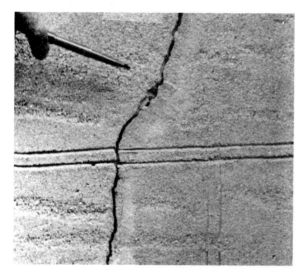

Fig. 62. Severe crack in basement wall.

Fig. 64. Crack in masonry wall.

Fig. 63. Wall patched and repaired.

Fig. 65. Acceptable masonry wall.

can also be cracked or the openings in the wall may be improperly sealed.

Step 1—Perform a visual examination of the basement walls. Check if they are cracked or if any opening in them has been poorly sealed. Refer to Figs. 62 and 63 for guidelines.

Are the walls cracked or is any opening poorl sealed?

YES—This condition is not only a serious heat-loss problem but in most cases is the cause of constant dampness in the basement. Refer to Figs. 64 and 65 for guidelines. Proceed to Step 2 for additional heat-loss checking.

NO—Proceed to Step 2.

Step 2—Insulation can be added to the inside of the basement walls which will help in reducing cold air seepage through the wall. This insulation will also be useful to contain the cool air in the house. Proceed to **1053** for continued basement heat-loss checks.

1053

Basement window losses

Basement windows can cause a great deal of heat loss. They should be examined for air penetration. Follow the check procedures of **1020**. When window inspection is completed, proceed to **1054** for additional heat-loss checks.

1054

Basement door losses

Basement doors can cause loss of heat in much the same manner as exterior house doors. For a thorough examination of basement doors and storm units, refer to **1010** and follow the steps therein. When examination is complete, proceed to **1060** for continued heat-loss checks.

After concluding the check procedures of **1051–1054,** the basement will be completely checked for heat losses. Should the you-fix-it home owner find that excessive air penetrations are still a problem, it is recommended that the home owner carefully retrace the steps of sections **1051–1054** to ascertain that nothing has been overlooked.

HEAT LOSS FROM EXTERIOR HOUSE WALLS

FAULT SYMPTOM 1060

Possible Causes:

- Cracks and jointing defects in outside walls ———— See **1061**
- Defects in seams and shingles ———————— See **1062**
- Insulation defect or omission from house walls ——————————————— See **1063**

Initial Conditions Check List:

a. Perform these checks on a cool or cold day when there is a strong breeze blowing. This will help make it easier to locate air leaks.

b. Stand at the interior of the house, at the exterior wall being checked, and note any excessive drafts or breezes that may be entering.

1061

Cracks and jointing defects in outside walls

A major cause of heat loss through exterior walls is cracks or loosened masonry joints. These faults allow excess air to penetrate into the house. Wherever air is able to penetrate, heat is being lost.

A

A

B

B

Fig. 66. Exterior walls.
  (A) Severe crack in concrete wall.
  (B) Open joints in masonry wall.

Fig. 67. Corrected exterior walls.
  (A) Properly pointed masonry joints.
  (B) Good concrete wall has no cracks visible.

Step 1—Examine the house from the outside, checking in particular all exterior walls. Look especially for cracks or open masonry jointing. Refer to Fig. 66A, B for guidelines.

Are there any cracks or open joints?

YES—Refer to Fig. 67A, B for repair guidelines. Your local masonry supplier can also provide some instruction and material selection assistance. Proceed to Step 2 for other heat-loss check steps.

NO—The interior, or house-side, of the exterior walls should be checked further, by running the palm of your hand along the walls. This will reveal if any cold air is penetrating from the outside. This is especially important to the home owner in determining if the walls have been insulated when the basement wall has finished panels and the insulation cannot be seen.

Is the interior side of the wall unusually cold?

YES—Proceed to Step 3.

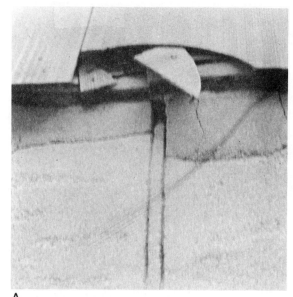

A

B

Fig. 68. Seams and shingles.
(A) Broken shingles cause heat loss.
(B) Loose and warped shingles should be firmly secured.

NO—The walls appear to be satisfactory. Proceed to **1062** for continuation of heat-loss checks.

Step 3—A more conclusive test for excessive temperature changes at the exterior walls is as follows. Place a thermometer on the inside face of the wall. Place another thermometer on an in-terior wall in the same room. The temperature difference between the two thermometers should not exceed five degrees. The exterior wall thermometer will record the lower temperature.

Is there a temperature difference in excess of five degrees?

YES—This is a good indication that the walls have not been insulated. Proceed to **1062** for continued heat-loss checks.

NO—Walls appear to be insulated properly. Proceed to **1062** for further heat-loss checks.

1062

Defects in seams and shingles

Heat loss through exterior walls can be due to air penetrating through loose shingles or seams.

Step 1—From outside the house, visually examine all exterior walls. Especially look for loose shingles and open seams as per the guidelines in Fig. 68A, B.

Are there loose shingles or open seams?

YES—Refer to Fig. 69 for repair guidelines. Proceed to Step 2 for additional checks.

NO—Proceed to Step 2.

Step 2—Run the palm of your hand along the inside house-side of the wall being checked. This will

Fig. 69. When shingle condition is good, all seams are tight and shingles are firmly secured.

help to establish whether cold air is being transferred through the outside house wall.

Does the wall feel unusually cold?

YES—Proceed to Step 3 of **1061** for checks of the walls, then to **1063**.

NO—Proceed to section **1063** for a continuation of heat-loss checking.

1063

Insulation defects or omission from exterior house walls

The largest amount of heat loss through exterior walls occurs when inside-the-wall insulation has been omitted (see Fig. 70).

Step 1—Inspect the outside walls of the house to see if insulation has been installed. Try to look into

Fig. 70. Removed switch box reveals that insulation (arrow) has been installed.

CAUTION
BE SURE TO SHUT DOWN ELECTRIC SUPPLY BEFORE REMOVING SWITCH BOX
CAUTION

the outer walls from an unfinished attic, the basement, or crawl space. Look down into the walls to see if there is insulation in the wall.

Can you see insulation?

YES—Proceed to **1070** for continuation of heat-loss checks.

NO—Proceed to Step 2.

Step 2—It will be necessary to verify the lack of insulation. Use a drill and make a few random holes along the sill in order to be able to see if insulation has been installed (see Figs. 70 and 71).

Has insulation been installed?

YES—Then proceed to **1070**.

NO—Insulation should be installed as soon as possible.

HEAT LOSS FROM FLOORS

Uninsulated floors over unfinished basements or crawl spaces contribute to heat-loss problems. The check steps outlined below will help locate floor heat-loss faults that may exist in the house (see Fig. 72).

Step 1—Examine the basement ceiling or the underside of a crawl space to establish whether insulation has been installed.

Has insulation been installed?

YES—Proceed to **1080** for additional heat-loss checking.

NO—Refer to manufacturers' installation instructions and Figs. 73 and 74. Then proceed to **1080** for continued heat-loss checking.

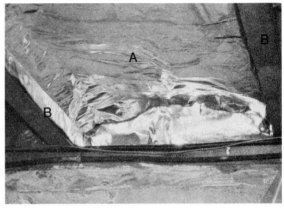

Fig. 73. Insulation (A) should cover wiring (shown in Fig. 74). Floor beams are (B).

Fig. 71. Drilling below exterior wall to locate insulation. (A) Basement floor beams; (B) concrete wall.

Fig. 74. Basement crawl space prior to installing insulation.

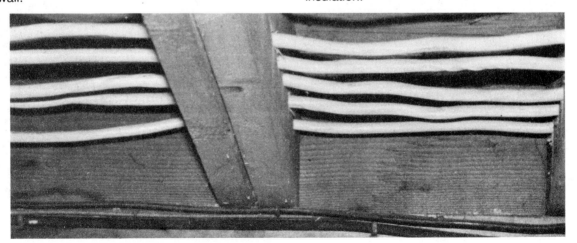

Fig. 72. An uninsulated basement and/or crawl space.

HEATING SYSTEMS

Inefficient heating systems can be a major cause of fuel loss. The you-fix-it home owner is advised to periodically check the home heating system in order to maintain its operation at peak efficiency (see Figs. 75 and 76). The following are a number of basic points the you-fix-it handyman should check.

1. Air systems have filters that require periodic changing. They should always be kept clean. Clean filters will reduce the work load of the heating plant, thus consuming less fuel. Locate the filters in your heating system, and keep a supply of clean filters handy (see Figs. 77 and 78).

Fig. 75. Typical hot air heating plant.

Fig. 76. Typical hot water heating plant.

Fig. 77. Dirty air filter for a hot air heating plant.

Fig. 78. Clean air filter for a hot air heating plant.

Keep a calendar near the heating plant. When the filters are changed, note the date of change on the calendar. For best results, change the filters three or four times each heating season.

2. Pilot lights in heating systems that have separate hot water units should be shut down during the summer (see Fig. 79). When these pilot lights are on all during warm periods they are simply wasteful and consume fuel. Also, the heat given off by these pilot lights adds an extra work load to any air conditioning or cooling equipment used in the home. Proceed to **4000** for suggested summer and winter maintenance procedures.

Fig. 79. Heating plant pilot lights (A) should be shut down during the periods that air conditioners are in use.

COST OF FUEL HEATING LOSS

Section 2000

Section **1000** discussed how and where to look for heating/fuel losses in the house. In this section, some typical examples of fuel and dollar losses are given for specific parts of the house where heat can be lost.

- Exterior door heating loss —————————— See **2001**
- Exterior window heat loss—double hung, wood sash windows —————————— See **2002**
- Exterior window heat loss—double hung, metal sash windows —————————— See **2003**
- Exterior window heat loss—steel casement windows —————————— See **2004**
- Convenience openings heatloss ————— See **2005**

2001

Exterior door heating loss

See Figs. 1 and 2 for a diagram of a typical, poorly fitting exterior door. As noted, the door *is not weatherstripped,* and *there is no storm door.* In the example which follows, the door size has been taken to be 3 feet wide by 6 feet 9 inches high. Heat loss for other doors may also be found by following this example. The amount of heat loss is directly dependent upon the difference between the inside and the outside temperatures. Heat loss also depends on whether the day is windy and how hard the wind is blowing. These factors have all been taken into account in calculations made by the authors. The results of these calculations are given in the line graphs of Figs. 80–85.

To find the heat loss for a poorly fitted exterior door, where there is no storm door, and which has no weatherstripping, proceed as follows.

Step 1—Determine the door size, height, and width. In this example the dimensions of the exterior door are as stated above: 3 feet wide by 6 feet 9 inches high.

Step 2—Determine the temperature difference between inside and outside the house. Your local radio station broadcasts the outside temperature regularly, or you can dial weather information on your telephone.

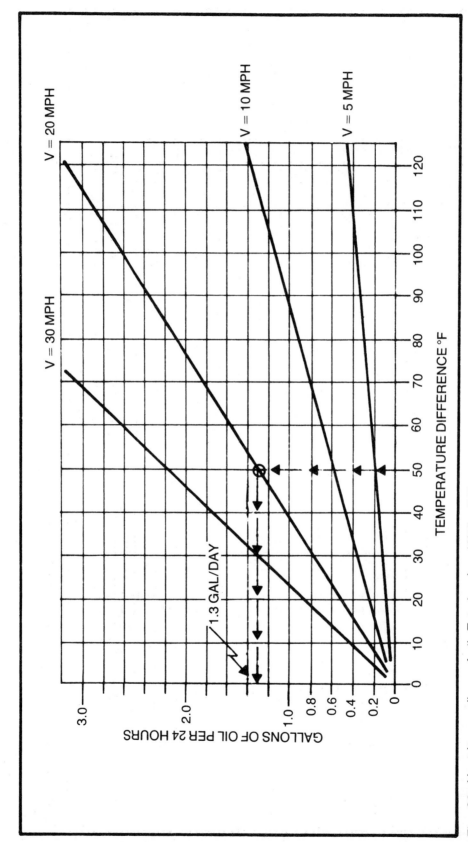

Fig. 80. Heat loss, gallons of oil. Exterior door: 3'0" x 6'9".

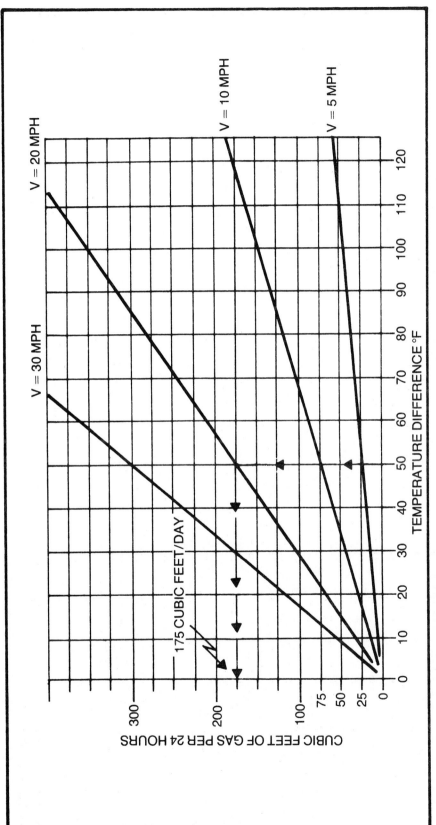

Fig. 81. Heat loss, cubic feet of gas. Exterior door: 3'0" x 6'9".

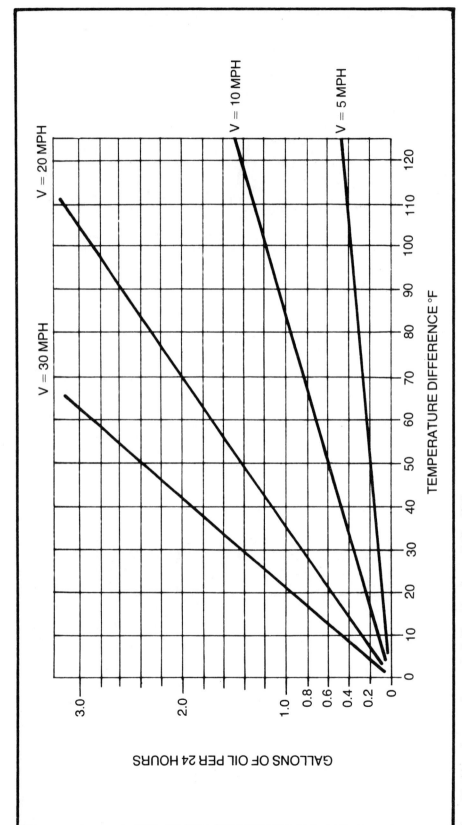

Fig. 82. Heat loss, gallons of oil. Exterior door: 3'6" x 6'9".

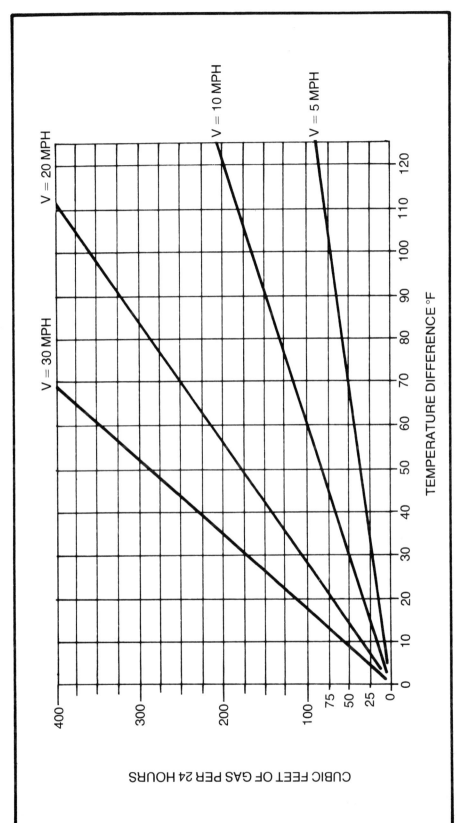

Fig. 83. Heat loss, cubic feet of gas. Exterior door: 3'6" x 6'9".

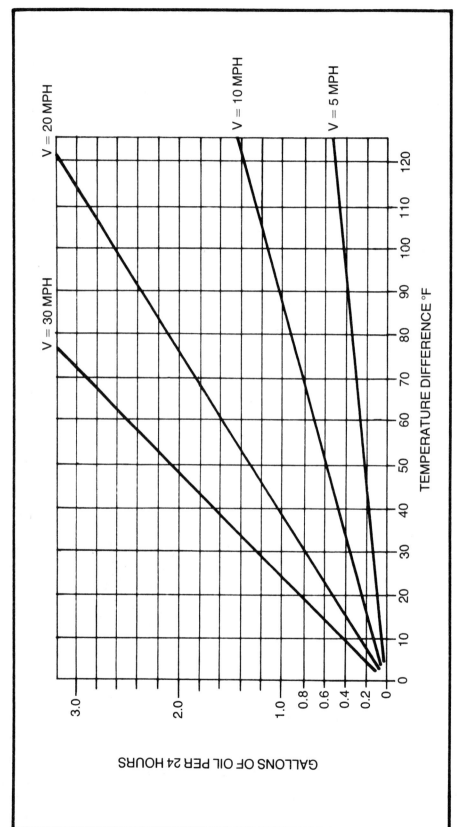

Fig. 84. Heat loss, gallons of oil. Exterior door: 3'6" x 6'9".

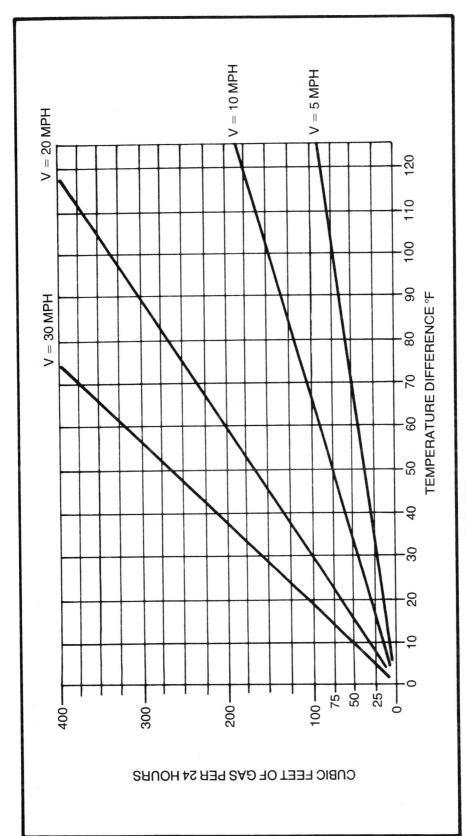

Fig. 85. Heat loss, cubic feet of gas. Exterior door: 3'6" x 6'9".

Step 3—Determine how hard the wind is blowing, to the closest 5 mph. (Again listen to your radio weather news.) Now select the wind velocity line on Fig. 80 which, for this example, is taken as 20 mph.

Step 4—Now, using the temperature difference from Step 2, for example 50°F, refer to Fig. 80, as shown at 50°F by the arrow▲. Follow the arrow straight up to the 20-mph line, then over to the left, as shown, and read the heat loss in gallons of oil per day—1.3 gallons in this case.

Step 5—In the same manner, heat losses can be found for higher wind values and/or greater or lesser temperature differences.

Step 6—If your home uses natural gas for heating instead of oil, follow the same procedure as in Step 4, except use Fig. 81. If we assume the same 20-mph wind outside and a 50°F temperature difference, then as per the example of Step 4, follow the arrow ▲ up to the 20-mph line. Proceed over to the left as shown, and read the heat loss in cubic feet of gas—175 cubic feet per day, in this case.

Step 7—Note that Figs. 80-87 give the heating loss for the size of the exterior door noted. If your home has a door for which there is no door size given, or is in between two of the sizes given, use the next larger size door figure. This will give a small error

and a bit higher than actual heat loss value. However, this error should not be significant.

2002

Exterior window heat loss—double hung, wood sash windows

To find the heat loss for a poorly fitted exterior, double hung, wooden sash window (where there is no storm window or weatherstripping) proceed as follows. In this example, a double mullion, 72 inches wide by 42 inches high; double hung wooden window will be used (see Fig. 86). This is really two windows placed side by side.

Fig. 86. Typical double mullion window.

Step 1—Determine the window size, in this case, 72 inches wide by 42 inches high, double mullion.

Step 2—Determine the temperature difference inside and outside the house and also the wind velocity outside. Your local radio weather station will advise on temperature and wind, or you can dial weather information on your telephone.

Step 3—In this example, we will assume a temperature difference of 60°F and a wind velocity of 20 mph. Go to Fig. 87 and enter the figure as shown by the arrow ⬆. Follow the arrow up to the 20-mph line and then over to the left, and read the heat loss in gallons of oil per day—1.0 gallons, in this case.

Step 4—Heat losses can be found in the same manner for higher or lower wind values and greater or lesser temperature differences. If the heat loss is desired in cubic feet of natural gas fuel, use Fig. 88.

Step 5—Figures, 87, 88, and 89–98 give the heating loss for specific wooden window types and sizes, such as single, California, etc. If the window you are checking is not among the sizes given, use the window size closest or next largest to your window. The resulting error should not be significant enough to make a big difference in your fuel loss.

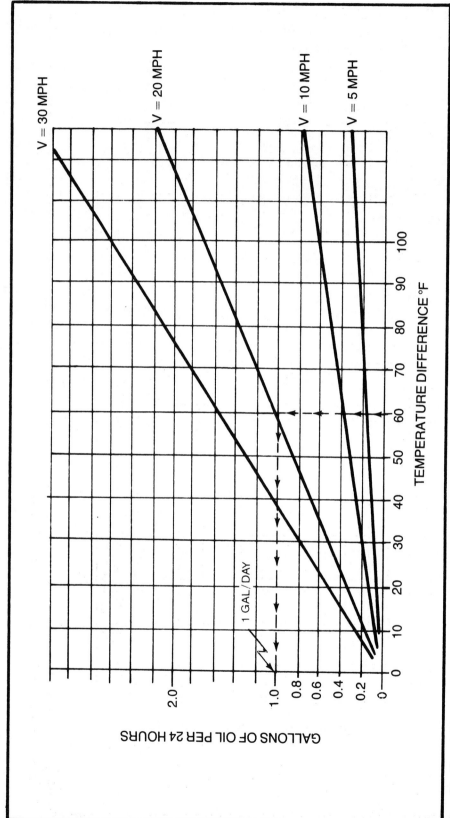

Fig. 87. Heat loss, gallons of oil. Double mullion window.

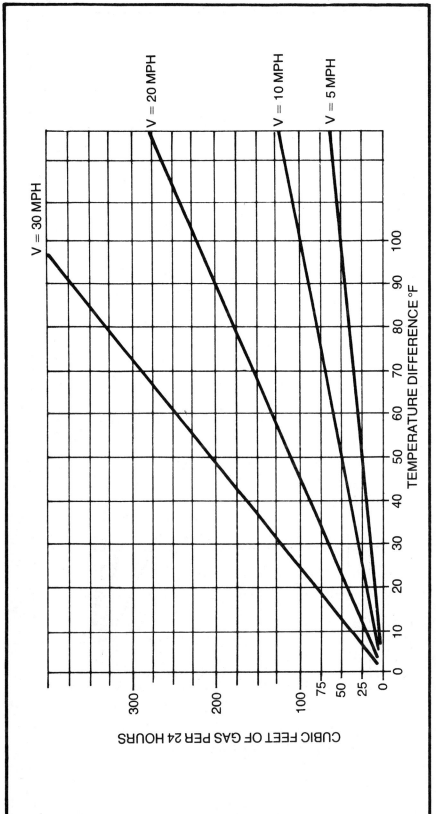

Fig. 88. Heat loss, cubic feet of gas. Double mullion window.

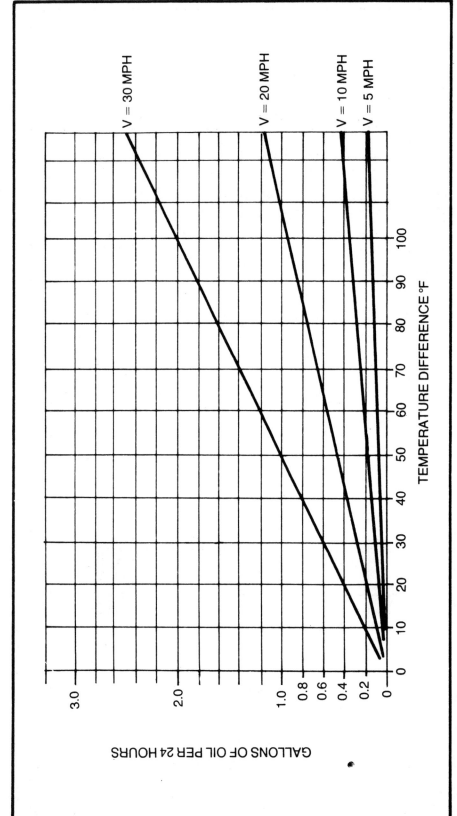

Fig. 89. Heat loss, gallons of oil. Single window: 36"W x 42"H.

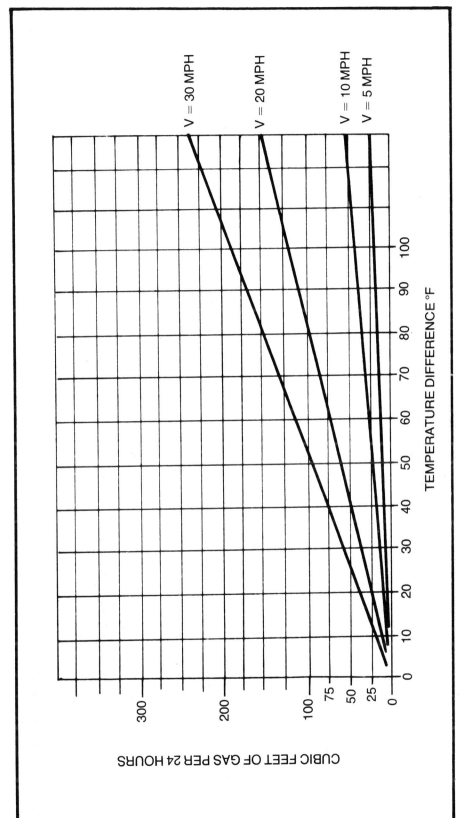

Fig. 90. Heat loss, cubic feet of gas. Single window: 36"W x 42"H.

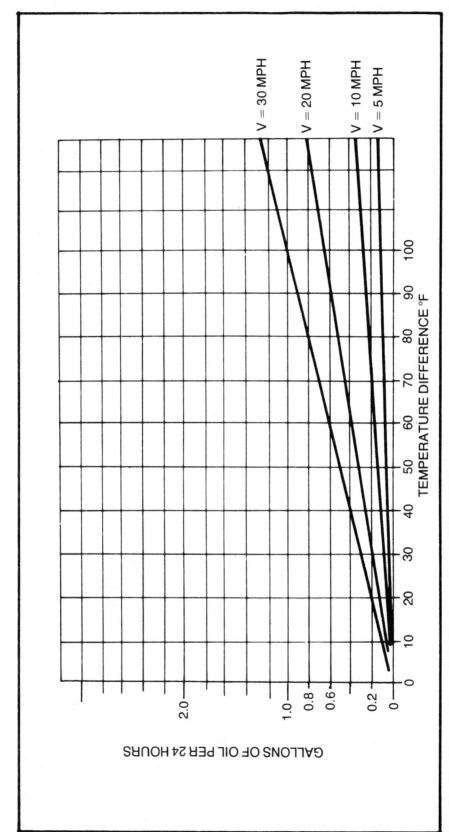

Fig. 91. Heat loss, gallons of oil. Single window: 24"W x 36"H.

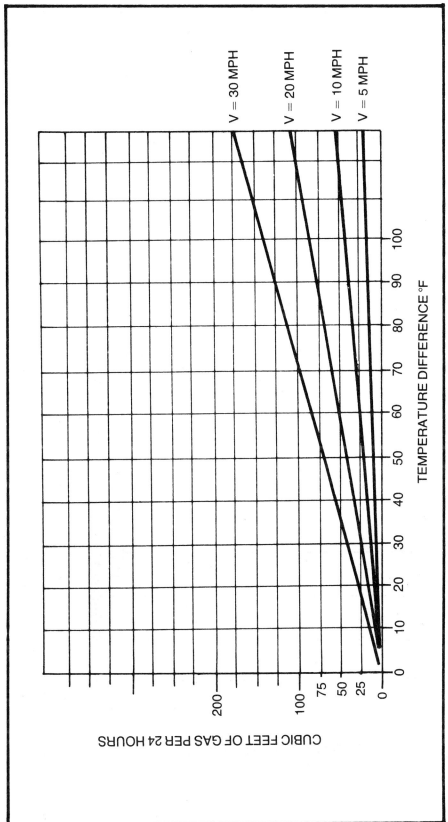

Fig. 92. Heat loss, cubic feet of gas. Single window: 24"W x 36"H.

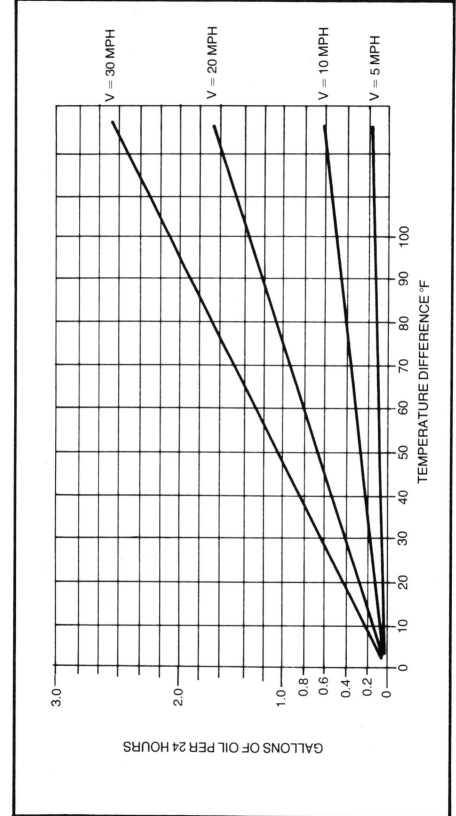

Fig. 93. Heat loss, gallons of oil. California window: 72''W x 48''H.

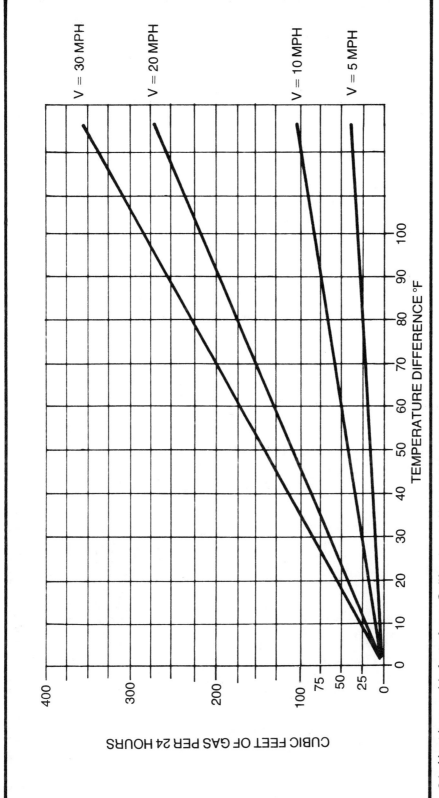

Fig. 94. Heat loss, cubic feet of gas. California window: 72"W x 48"H.

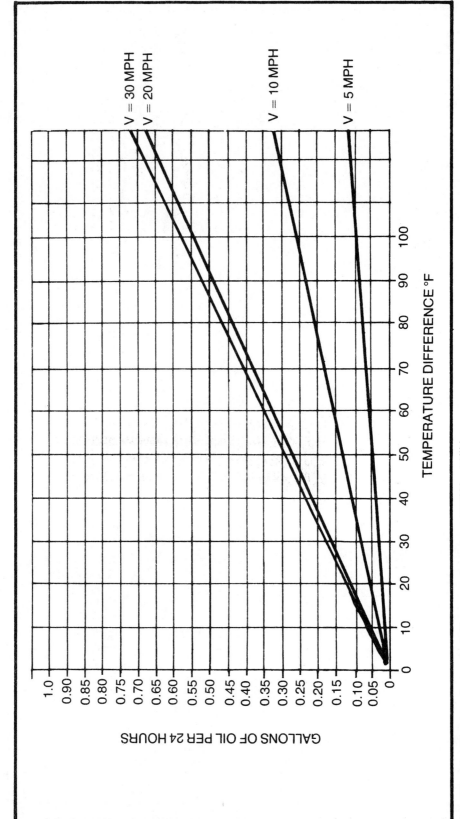

Fig. 95. Heat loss, gallons of oil. Basement window: 32"W x 16"H.

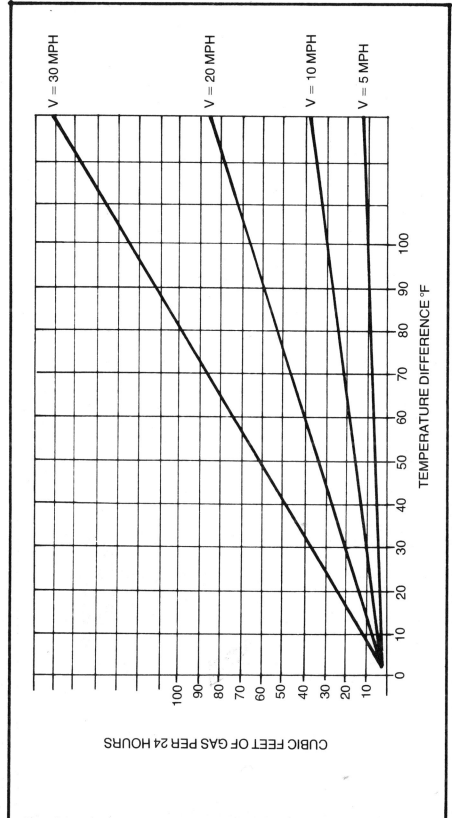

Fig. 96. Heat loss, cubic feet of gas. Basement window: 32"W x 16"H.

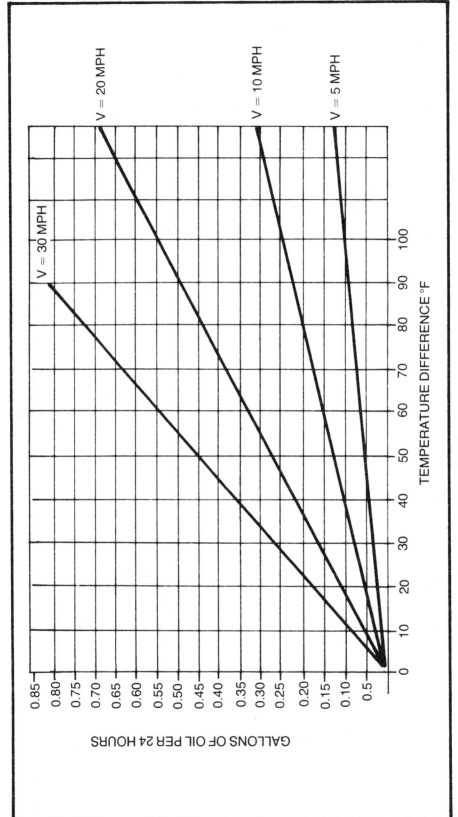

Fig. 97. Heat loss, gallons of oil. Basement window: 32"W x 20"H.

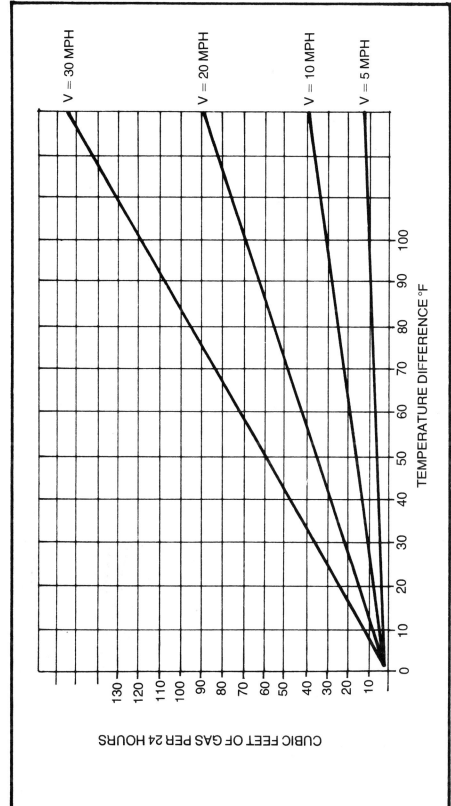

Fig. 98. Heat loss, cubic feet of gas. Basement window: 32"W x 20"H.

2003

Exterior window heat loss—double hung, metal sash windows

Exterior double hung metal sash windows, even though not weatherstripped, have a lower loss due to cold outside air infiltration than the wood sash windows discussed in **2002.** Although this heat loss will vary with the type of double hung metal sash window, the home owner with this type of window will lose about 40 percent less fuel oil, or natural gas, for a given metal window than will one with the same wooden window. To find the heat loss for an unlocked closed, double hung metal sash window, proceed as follows.

Step 1—Follow the steps given in **2002** for finding the heat loss in gallons of oil or in cubic feet of gas for a comparable wooden window. Then take 60 percent of that number. This is your heat loss for the double hung metal sash window.

NOTE

If double hung wooden window loss is 1.0 gallon, then 60 percent $\times$ 1.0 = 0.6 gallon, the heat loss for the double hung metal window.

2004

Exterior window heat loss—steel casement windows

Casement windows used for residential purposes are generally rolled section steel sash and, without weatherstripping, provide a lower heat loss to cold outside air infiltration than the wooden sash discussed in **2002.** The heat loss for steel casement windows will be about 50 per-

cent lower than for the wooden sash. Therefore, to find the heat loss for an unlocked closed steel casement window as shown in Fig. 99, simply find the loss for the comparable oversize wooden window from Figs. 89-98 and take one-half of that value.

Fig. 99. Typical steel casement window.

2005

Convenience openings heat loss

Some houses have small access openings such as trap doors, small cellar doors, or other types of openings to confined spaces normally used for dead storage or to permit inspection. Basement crawl spaces sometimes contain a smaller exterior access opening which is covered over by a wooden frame or cover. These convenience openings are sources of heat loss. The heat lost in gallons of fuel oil or natural gas for some representative access area openings can be found as follows.

Step 1—Refer to Figs. 100–107 and find the size opening which is closest to the access opening in your house. If the exact size is not listed, select the next larger size. If the access opening is larger than those presented in the figures, use Fig. 106 (or 107) and add a percentage between that figure and the access opening.

NOTE

If the access opening is 50 percent larger than that in Fig. 106, add 50 percent to the value as found in Fig. 106.

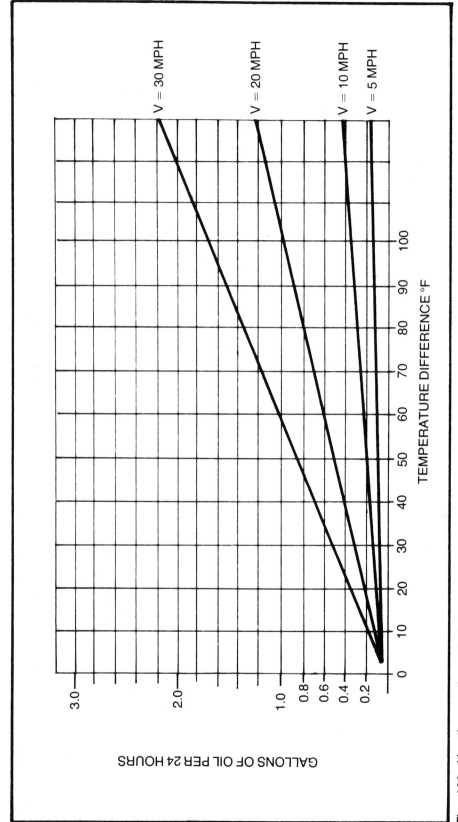

Fig. 100. Heat loss, gallons of oil. Access openings: 24" x 24".

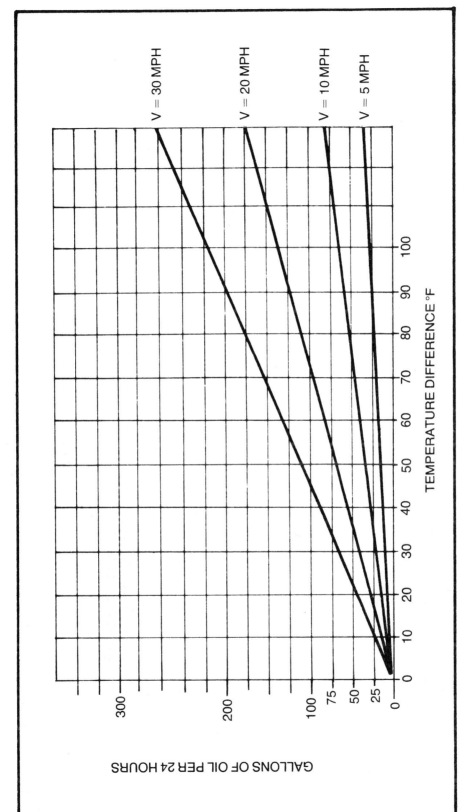

Fig. 101. Heat loss, cubic feet of gas. Access openings: 24" x 24".

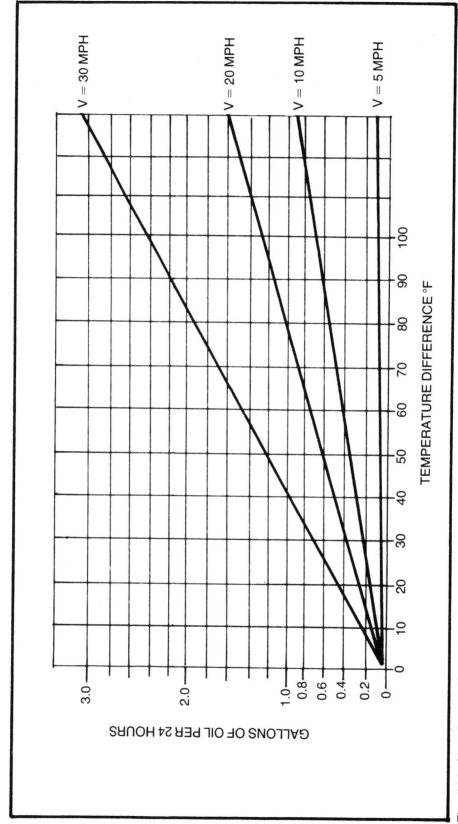

Fig. 102. Heat loss, gallons of oil. Access openings: 24"W x 36"H.

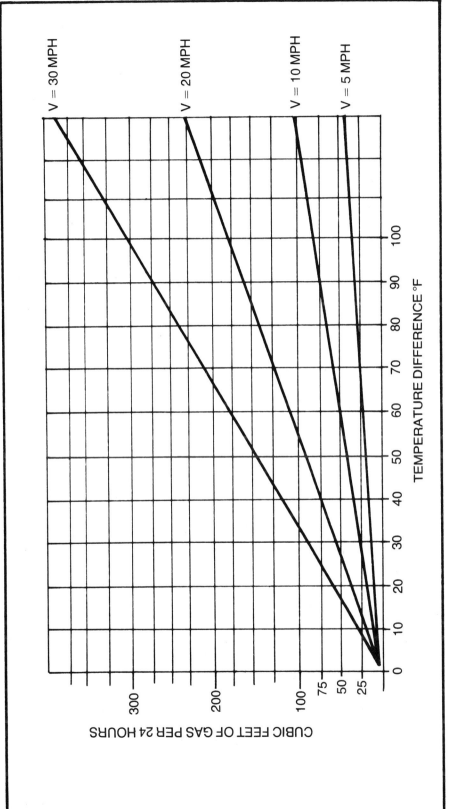

Fig. 103. Heat loss, cubic feet of gas. Access openings 24"W x 36"H.

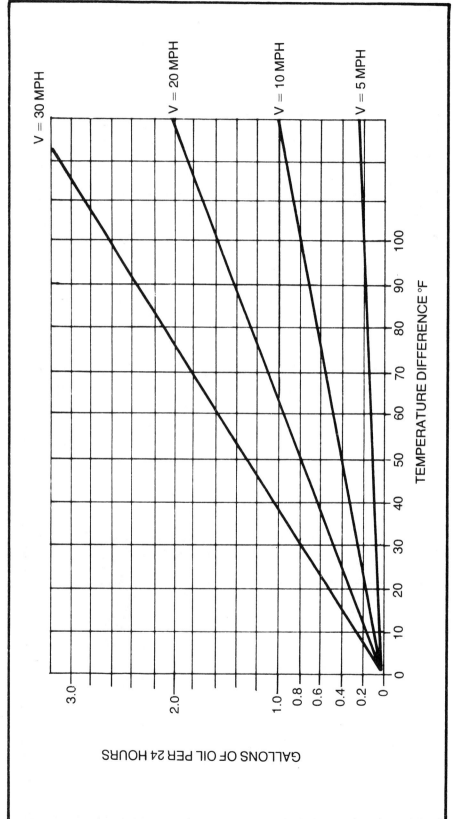

Fig. 104. Heat loss, gallons of oil. Access openings: 24"W x 48"H.

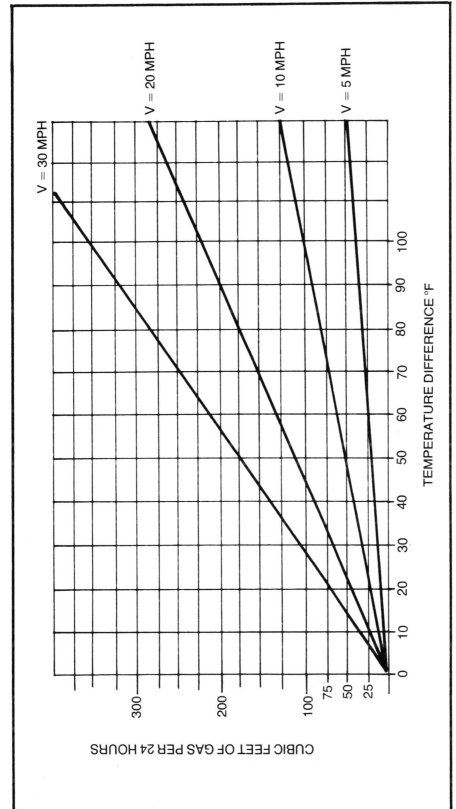

Fig. 105. Heat loss, cubic feet of gas. Access openings: 24"W x 48"H.

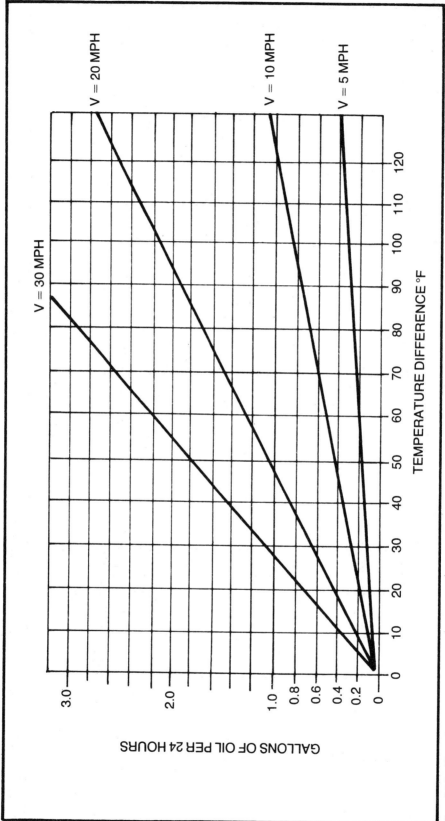

Fig. 106. Heat loss, gallons of oil. Access openings: 48" x 48".

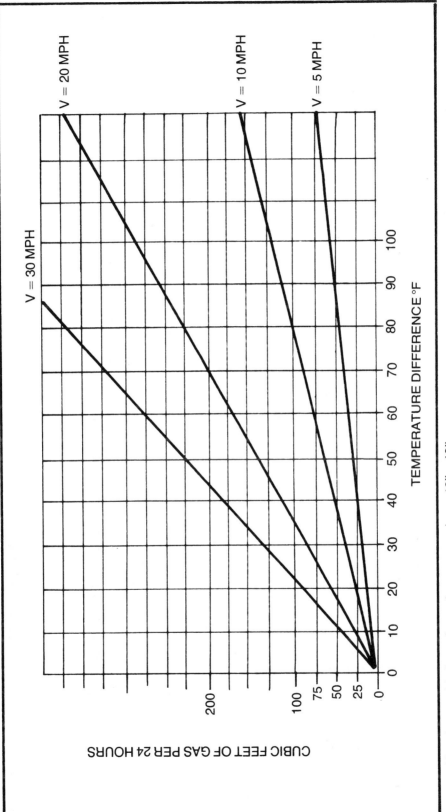

Fig. 107. Heat loss, cubic feet of gas. Access openings: 48" x 48".

HEAT LOSS COSTS AND COSTS OF REPAIR

SECTION 3000

Sections **1000** and **2000** provided the means to inspect and locate points of fuel heat losses in the home and estimates of the dollar costs of such losses. This section provides the home owner with a heat-loss cost tabulation which can be used for heat-loss areas of the house. Individual dollar losses may be found for specific areas (doors or windows) and the total dollar loss added up for the entire house. Upon establishing the heat-loss cost (or costs when multiple problems exist), this dollar cost can be compared with the estimated cost of repair: to fix or not to fix. In all but a few cases, the

cost to fix will repay itself in a very short time, thereby making the repair a sound investment. Additionally, eliminating uncomfortable areas, such as drafty windows, contributes a great deal to a pleasant and comfortable home.

Costs of repairing and replacing are found in Table I. The heat loss or source of the loss is given, and nominal costs for one severe winter month using either oil or gas fuel are presented. Using Table I, the do-it-yourself home owner can decide whether or not to correct the heat loss.

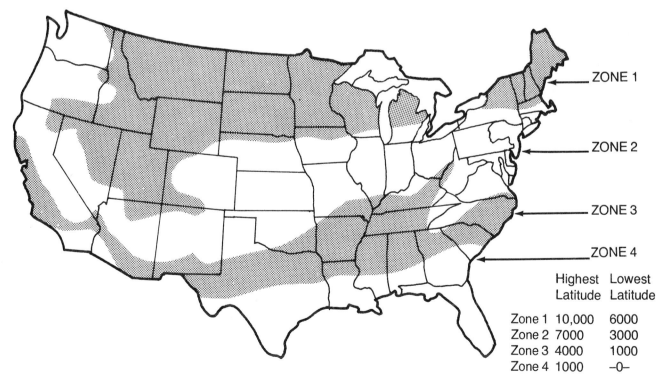

	Highest Latitude	Lowest Latitude
Zone 1	10,000	6000
Zone 2	7000	3000
Zone 3	4000	1000
Zone 4	1000	–0–

Fig. 108. Typical heating season. Range of degree days for United States geographic areas.

TABLE I.

Tabulation of Home Heat Loss Costs

HEAT LOSS SOURCE	ESTIMATED ONE MONTH COST[1]		ESTIMATED COST TO FIX	COMMENT/ANALYSIS FIX VS. NOT FIX
	FUEL LOSS OIL $0.40/gal	Gas $0.01/ft[3]		
Exterior Door No weather seals Or defective weatherseals With defective caulking Without storm door	(for nominal) 3' x 6'9" door[2] $10.40 per month	$29.50 per month	Weatherseal plus caulking; about $18 per door	Repair cost will be repaid by fuel/oil cost saved in less than two months
Exterior Door Same as above, but with a storm door added	$5.20 per month	$14.75 per month	Weatherseal, caulking, plus a new storm door; about $75 per door	Cost will be repaid (oil) in approximately one heating season
Exterior Window No weatherseals Or defective weatherseals	Single 36" x 42" window; $5.60 per month[3]	$10.00 per month	Weatherseal plus caulking; about $16 per window	Repair cost will be repaid by fuel saved (oil) in about four months
With defective caulking	Double mullion (double window) 42" x 72" window $10.40 per month	$18.50 per month	Weatherseal plus caulking; about $20 per window	Cost repaid by fuel (oil) saved in less than two months
Without storm window	Basement windows 16" x 32" $0.96	$5.90 per month	Weatherseal plus caulking; about $8 per window	Repair cost repaid (oil) in about one heating season
Exterior Window Same as above, but with a storm window added	Single window; $2.80 per month	$5.00 per month	Weatherseal, caulking, plus a new storm window; $40 per window	Repair cost repaid (oil) in two heating seasons
	Double mullion; $5.20 per month	$9.25 per month	Weatherseal, caulking, plus a new storm window; $68	Repair cost repaid (oil) in approximately one heating season
	Basement window; $0.50 per month	$4.50 per month	Weatherseal, caulking, plus a new storm window; $24	Repair cost repaid (oil) after eight heating seasons
Convenience Openings	(for nominal 2' x 2' opening[4]); $4.00 per month	$11.50 per month	Weatherseal plus caulking; about $16	Repair cost repaid in four months by fuel saved
access openings	(for nominal 2' x 3' opening[5]); $5.60 per month	$14.50 per month	Weatherseal plus caulking; about $15—plus cloth cover $8—total $23	Repair cost repaid in about four months by fuel saved

	Approximately $1.00 per month (3 openings) / Estimated Annual Fuel Loss Cost[5]	Approx. $2.00 per month (3 openings)	Caulk and seal off; about $10 / Install insulation	Repair cost repaid in less than two heating seasons
Wall air conditioner opening pipe/electric line utility entries	Approximately $1.00 per month (3 openings)	Approx. $2.00 per month (3 openings)	Caulk and seal off; about $10	Repair cost repaid in less than two heating seasons
House Walls Exterior—No Insulation	Estimated Annual Fuel Loss Cost[5]			
Wood frame wall (shingles or clapboard)	$40 per 1000 square feet of uninsulated wall area		Install insulation approximately $200 (@ $0.20 per square foot installed)	Repair cost will be repaid by fuel (oil) cost saved in five heating seasons
Wood frame. brickveneer wall	$55 per 1000 square feet of uninsulated wall area		Same as above	Same as above
Brickwall (8" brick. or 8" cinder block)	$57 per 1000 square feet of uninsulated wall area		Same as above	same as above
House Attic No insulation in attic. vented attic	$140 per 1000 square feet of uninsulated attic floor area		Install insulation approximately $200 (@ $0.20 per square foot installed)	Repair cost will be repaid by fuel (oil) cost saved in less than two heating seasons
With attic insulation, and with no weathersealed attic windows and/or attic doors, or attic trapdoor	See above on windows and doors—fuel loss costs are approximately the same			
House Basement Wood frame floor over unheated basement; no floor insulation	$45 per 1000 squre feet of uninsulated floor area		Install insulation approximately $200 (@ $0.20 per square foot installed)	Repair cost will be repaid by fuel (oil) cost saved in about five heating seasons
Basement windows and/or doors	See above on windows and doors loss			

1 Cost computed on basis of one (1) severe winter month of 30 days. Assume 10 days with wind velocity 20 mph and Δ Temp. 50°, remainder of 20 days velocity 10 mph and Δ Temp. 40°. For an accurate, actual cost, the reader must maintain a daily wind and Δ Temp. log and calculate fuel costs from the appropriate figure given. Fuel costs per unit are for the New York Metropolitan Area, Winter 1974–75. Gas unit cost assumed as nominal for residential heating, which varies with quantity used.

2 For other size doors, refer to appropriate figure for daily fuel loss cost.

3 For other size windows, refer to appropriate figure for daily fuel loss cost.

4 For other size openings, refer to appropriate figure for daily fuel loss cost.

5 Cost predicated on basis of moderate cold weather zone for New York Metropolitan Area with annual 6000 degree days. (Degree days are number of days when average daily temperature is below 65°F. Product of number of degrees below 65 and number of days equals degree days.) For higher degree days (or lower), use a direct scaling proportion for cost. See Fig. 108 for degree days in your geographic region.

SUMMER AND WINTER SUGGESTED MAINTENANCE PROCEDURES

SECTION 4000

SUMMER MAINTENANCE

SERVICE PROCEDURE 4010

4011

Heating plants

1. Heating plants that are not employed to produce domestic hot water should be shut down during the summer period (see Fig. 109).

2. Shut off all pilot lights that are not required for hot water, oven heat, etc. (see Fig. 110).

3. Shut off all electrical switches and motors not required to operate air conditioning units or lights (see Fig. 111).

4. Be sure to shut OFF the electrical switch used in the operation of the heating unit (see Fig. 111).

Fig. 109. Shut down heating plant (A) during summer, especially if a separate hot water heater (B) is used.

Fig. 110. Be sure to shut off pilot light in heating plant.

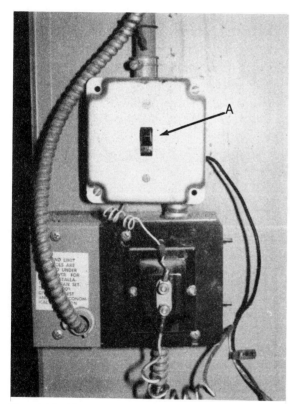

Fig. 111. Be sure all electric switches (A) and motors not required for air conditioning units or lights are shut OFF.

4012

Storm window and door units

1. Check all the caulking and weather-stripping at all door and window storm units to ascertain that they are in sufficiently good condition to help keep heat out and cool air in. See Figs. 21 and 112.

2. Check to be sure that all screening has been installed in the storm units and that the screening is in good condition.

3. In cases where a central air conditioning unit is employed, be sure that all the storm units are airtight. This

Fig. 112. Make certain that all caulking and weatherstripping at storm units are in good condition.

Fig. 113. Increased efficiency occurs when air conditioning filters are kept clean.
(A) Layers of dirt and dust.
(B) Clean air conditioner filter.

will cut down on the work load of the air conditioning unit and keep it operating at peak efficiency for a longer period of time.

4013

Air conditioning units

1. Be sure to periodically clean all filters for air conditioning units in order to cut down on the operating time of the unit (see Fig. 113A, B).

2. Be sure all motors are operating at peak performance. Motors should be oiled periodically (or checked if they are permanently sealed units; see Fig. 114).

Fig. 114. Oil motors regularly to keep them operating at peak performance.

Fig. 115. Be certain to remove all air conditioner unit covers.

3. Air conditioning refrigerant should be checked to ascertain that the proper amount is maintained.

4. Be sure all winter covers have been removed from the air conditioning units prior to turning the units on (see Fig. 115).

4014

Caulking and jointing

1. Check the caulking around all windows and doors, convenience openings, etc. Be sure it has not been damaged by the elements during the winter. Repair or replace any caulking or jointing as required (see Figs. 116 and 117).

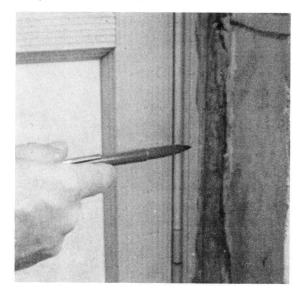

Fig. 116. Caulking that needs replacing.

Fig. 118. Check framework jointing and caulking.

Fig. 117. Accessory opening that is properly caulked.

2. Check all framework and masonry jointing to be sure it has not deteriorated over the winter months (see Figs. 118 and 119).

3. Properly sealed openings will help keep cool air in the house, thereby reducing the working time of the cooling units.

Fig. 119. Check for poor masonry caulking.

4015

Blinds and shades

1. Make certain that all blinds or shades are in good condition and kept closed. This will keep down the sun's heat through the windows (see Figs. 120 and 121).

4016

Weatherstripping

1. All weatherstripping should be checked to be sure it is in satisfactory condition (see Figs. 122 and 123).

2. Replace any weatherstripping that has deteriorated from the elements during the winter months.

4017

Fans

1. Remove all winter covers from fans in order that they may operate properly (see Fig. 124).

2. Be sure that all fan motors are in operating condition and have been properly serviced. Do not forget to oil the motors (see Fig. 116).

Fig. 120. Shades help keep the hot sun out of the house.

Fig. 121. Blinds should be close-fitting to help keep the sun's heat from overworking air conditioning units.

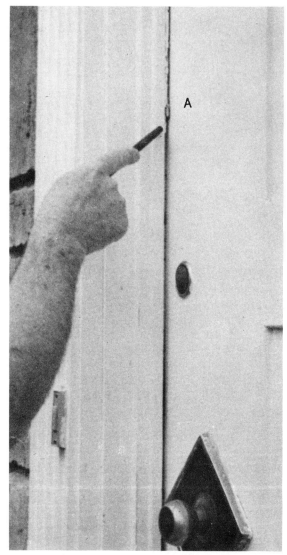

Fig. 122. Missing weatherstripping (A) will keep air conditioning units working longer.

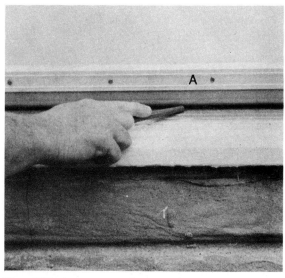

Fig. 123. Loose weather seals consume extra energy. Note space at door sill weatherstripping (A).

Fig. 124. All covers must be removed from fan units prior to operating.

WINTER MAINTENANCE

SERVICE PROCEDURE 4020

4021

Heating plants

1. Maker certain the heating plant has been turned on and there is enough fuel to operate the unit.

2. Turn ON all pilot lights that were shut down during the summer.

3. Be sure that all electrical switches and motors required to operate the heating plant are turned ON.

4022

Drapery

The addition of heavy drapery at windows will greatly reduce air penetration.

4023

Weatherstripping

All weatherstripping should be checked to be sure it is in satisfactory condition. Any faulty weatherstripping must either be replaced or repaired. This will reduce heat loss.

4024

Storm units

1. Check all the caulking and weatherstripping at door and window storm units to ascertain that they are in good condition and will keep cold air infiltration to a minimum.

2. Check to be sure that all screening has been replaced with glass sections in the storm units and that the glass units are in good condition.

4025

Caulking and jointing

1. Check the caulking around all windows, doors, convenience openings, etc. Be sure it has not deteriorated from the summer heat. Repair or replace any caulking or jointing as required.

2. Check all framework and masonry jointing to be sure it is in good condition.

3. Properly sealed openings will help keep warm air in the house.

4026

Fans

1. Be sure all fan motors have been shut off.

2. Check to make certain that all winter fan covers have been installed.

4027

Air conditioning units

1. Be sure all air conditioning units have been shut down for the winter.

2. Make certain winter covers have been installed where required.

INDEX

Fault symptom number appears in boldface; page number in lightface.

YOU FIX IT SERIES

In this period of ever-rising service costs, this unusual new series of books, which provides step-by-step instruction for repairing and maintaining appliances with tools readily available in the average home workshop, is an economic necessity for every household's budget.

By following four carefully outlined steps—malfunction verification, fault isolation, maintenance and service procedures, then post maintenance and service checks—even the unskilled man or woman can avoid costly professional repairs and fix common household appliances themselves. Each YOU FIX IT book starts with what is known—a symptom, such as "the engine won't start"—and then continues through an easy-to-follow procedure of what to do and how to do it. No prior knowledge or mechanical background is required.

Each paperbound volume in the series contains over 150 photographs or drawings. Each book is $4.95.

YOU FIX IT: **LAWN MOWERS**

YOU FIX IT: **PLUMBING**

YOU FIX IT: **WASHING MACHINES**

YOU FIX IT: **CLOTHES DRYERS** (Electric and Gas)

YOU FIX IT: **INSULATION** ($3.95)

YOU FIX IT: **SMALL APPLIANCES**

Purchase these books at your bookstore: or send $4.95 per book (plus 35¢ each book, postage and handling) to

ARCO PUBLISHING COMPANY, INC.

219 Park Ave. South, New York, N.Y. 10003

ARCO "HOW-TO" BOOKS

Each Book, Like This One, Shows You Exactly How-To-Do-It Yourself.
Each Book, Like This One, The Very Best In Its Field. Each Is Carefully
Edited, Beautifully Library Bound In Cloth With "Show-How" Illustrations.

THE NEW COMPLETE WOODWORKING HANDBOOK

Jeanette T. Adams and Emanuele Stieri

Written for the lay woodworker, the book is also useful to the skilled craftsman who wants to keep up to date on the subject. Full instructions are provided on all types of wood, hand- and power-driven tools, paints and finishes, repairs, projects, glues, etc.
"Comprehensive instruction and reference book that covers the entire field of woodworking."—*Industrial Reports and Publications.*

900 illustrations; indexed;
5½" x 8½"; 576 pages
LR cloth $8.95

HANDYMAN'S CONCRETE AND MASONRY HANDBOOK

R. J. de Cristoforo

Chapters include making good concrete, brick-laying, building walks and driveways. There are plans for construction of a concrete block garage and a family swimming pool. Every vital phase of concrete and masonry work is clearly and concisely covered.

Illustrated; 6" x 9"; 114 pages
cloth $3.95

THE ARCO WORKSHOP COMPANION

W. Oakley

One hundred seventy-nine detailed sections to aid the home craftsman set up his workshop; learn how to buy good tools, use and maintain them; and how to work with wood and metal. W. Oakley is a faculty member of Prestwood Lodge School.

322 illustrations; indexed;
5½" x 8½"; 218 pages
cloth $3.50

HOW TO USE TOOLS

Alfred Morgan

Introduces the reader to hand tools, names parts, enumerates functions, and shows the right way to employ basic instruments. Easy-to-understand text, and step-by-step photographs.

Illustrated; 6½" x 9½";
144 pages
LR cloth $3.50

HANDY MAN'S PLUMBING AND HEATING GUIDE

Larry Eisinger, Ed.

Clearly explains how to handle every eventuality around the home, with simple text and over 300 photos and illustrations. Sixty subjects are covered, each one of which make the book invaluable.

Illustrated; 6½" x 9½";
144 pages
LR cloth $3.95

HOW TO BUILD AND BUY CABINETS FOR THE MODERN KITCHEN

R. P. Stevenson

Completely revised and up-to-date edition of this classic includes such items as the familiar Lazy Susan mounted in corner cabinets, shelves that slide in and out to make stored items easier to find or reach, sinks placed across a corner, sliding shelves that stand on edge, pull-out racks, space-saving dining centers and dozens of other cabinet suggestions—most of them with clear, easy-to-follow working drawings. In addition, many photographs illustrate the latest developments in kitchen design.

Photographs, line drawings;
index; 8" x 10½"; 272 pages
cloth $10.00

REFINISHING FURNITURE

W. H. Kuhn

How to finish and refinish all types of furniture is illustrated with how-to photos and step-by-step instructions. The book also tells how to repair and remodel old furniture before giving it a new finish, how to remove old finishes and prepare the wood for a fine new finish, and how to work with clear, painted and specialty finishes.

Over 300 illustrations;
6¼" x 9¼"; 108 pages
LR cloth $4.95

ARCO PUBLISHING COMPANY, INC.

219 Park Avenue South, New York, N.Y. 10003